Scott, Foresman

Science

Series Consultant

Irwin L. Slesnick
Department of Biology
Western Washington University
Bellingham, Washington

Program Consultant

Ronald D. Anderson
Laboratory for Research
in Science and Mathematics Education
University of Colorado
Boulder, Colorado

Reading Consultant

Robert A. Pavlik
Reading-Language Arts Department
Cardinal Stritch College
Milwaukee, Wisconsin

Special Writers

Laboratories
Alfred DeVito
Science Education
Purdue University
Lafayette, Indiana

Enrichment Features
David Newton
Department of Chemistry
Salem State College
Salem, Massachusetts

Authors

Michael R. Cohen
School of Education
Indiana University
Indianapolis, Indiana

Bette J. Del Giorno
Science Consultant
Fairfield Public Schools
Fairfield, Connecticut

Jean Durgan Harlan
Education Division
University of Wisconsin, Parkside
Kenosha, Wisconsin

Alan J. McCormack
Science and Mathematics
Teaching Center
College of Education
University of Wyoming
Laramie, Wyoming

John R. Staver
College of Education and
College of Liberal Arts and Sciences
University of Illinois at Chicago
Chicago, Illinois

Cover: Gila woodpeckers live in desert regions of the southwestern United States and northern Mexico. They are often found near saguaros.

Scott, Foresman and Company
Editorial Offices: Glenview, Illinois

Regional Offices: Palo Alto, California
Tucker, Georgia • Glenview, Illinois
Oakland, New Jersey • Dallas, Texas

Reviewers and Contributors

Gretchen M. Alexander
Program Coordinator
Museum of Science and Industry
Chicago, Illinois

Daniel W. Ball
Division of Education
Northeast Missouri State University
Kirksville, Missouri

Mary Coban
Teacher
Divine Savior School
Norridge, Illinois

Thomas Graika
Science Chairman
School District 102
LaGrange, Illinois

Robert G. Guy
Science Teacher
Big Lake Elementary School
Sedro Woolley, Washington

Irma G. Hamilton
Science Teacher
Oglethorpe Elementary School
Atlanta, Georgia

Judy Haney
Teacher
East Noble School Corporation
Kendallville, Indiana

Garth P. Harris
Teacher
Lincoln Elementary School
Evanston, Illinois

Edwina Hill
Principal
Oglethorpe Elementary School
Atlanta, Georgia

LaVerne Jackson, Sr.
Science Teacher
Medgar Evers Elementary School
Chicago, Illinois

Hollis R. Johnson
Astronomy Department
Indiana University
Bloomington, Indiana

Irene S. Kantner
Teacher
Lincoln Elementary School
Evanston, Illinois

Sol Krasner
Department of Physics
University of Chicago
Chicago, Illinois

Dolores Mann
Teacher
Glenview Public Schools
Glenview, Illinois

Phillip T. Miyazawa
Instructional Consultant
Science Education
Denver Public Schools
Denver, Colorado

Anita E. Moore
Principal
George Howland Elementary School
Chicago, Illinois

Janet Ostrander
Teacher
Indian Trail School
Highland Park, Illinois

Barbara Scott
Teacher
Crown Magnet School
Chicago, Illinois

Elaine R. Seaman
Teacher
Greenbrier Elementary School
Arlington Heights, Illinois

R. A. Slotter
Department of Chemistry
Northwestern University
Evanston, Illinois

Anita Snell
Coordinator of Primary Education
Spring Branch Independent
School District
Houston, Texas

Lois Spangler
Teacher
Central School
Great Meadows, New Jersey

Carol Leth Stone
Biology Writer
Stanford, California

Johanna F. Strange
Model Laboratory School
Eastern Kentucky University
Richmond, Kentucky

William D. Thomas
Science Supervisor
Escambia County Schools
Pensacola, Florida

Dorothy Wallinga
Christian Schools International
Grand Rapids, Michigan

Les Wallinga
Science Teacher
Calvin Christian Junior High School
Wyoming, Michigan

ISBN: 0-673-14003-2

Copyright © 1984, Scott, Foresman and Company, Glenview, Illinois. All rights Reserved. Printed in the United States of America.

12345678910 KPK 9291908988887868585483

When You Read This Book

1 Read the question.

3 Find the answer.

4 Learn the science words.

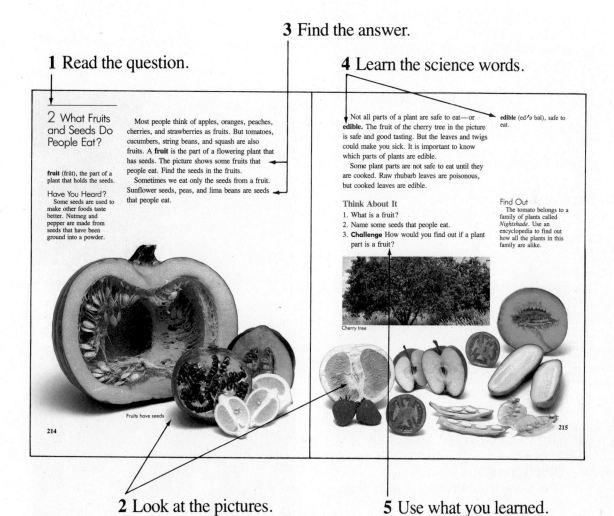

2 What Fruits
and Seeds Do
People Eat?

fruit (früt), the part of a
plant that holds the seeds.

Have You Heard?
Some seeds are used to
make other foods taste
better. Nutmeg and
pepper are made from
seeds that have been
ground into a powder.

Most people think of apples, oranges, peaches,
cherries, and strawberries as fruits. But tomatoes,
cucumbers, string beans, and squash are also
fruits. A **fruit** is the part of a flowering plant that
has seeds. The picture shows some fruits that
people eat. Find the seeds in the fruits.

Sometimes we eat only the seeds from a fruit.
Sunflower seeds, peas, and lima beans are seeds
that people eat.

Not all parts of a plant are safe to eat—or
edible. The fruit of the cherry tree in the picture
is safe and good tasting. But the leaves and twigs
could make you sick. It is important to know
which parts of plants are edible.

Some plant parts are not safe to eat until they
are cooked. Raw rhubarb leaves are poisonous,
but cooked leaves are edible.

edible (ed′ə bəl), safe to
eat.

Think About It
1. What is a fruit?
2. Name some seeds that people eat.
3. **Challenge** How would you find out if a plant
   part is a fruit?

Find Out
The tomato belongs to a
family of plants called
Nightshade. Use an
encyclopedia to find out
how all the plants in this
family are alike.

Cherry tree

Fruits have seeds

214

215

2 Look at the pictures.

5 Use what you learned.

Unit One Your Body's Needs

Unit Two Light and Sound

Unit Three Magnetism and Electricity

Unit Four The Earth Beneath Our Feet

Unit Five Fossils

Unit Six Water

Chapter 11
Water and the Weather *150*

Chapter 12
Water, Water Everywhere *158*

Unit Seven Protection and Defense in Living Things

Unit Eight Green and Growing

UNIT ONE YOUR BODY'S NEEDS

Sliding on the water
Happy, sliding, splashing.
Warm, cool, slippery water.
Afternoon of summer.

Eddilyne Bahyesva *age 8*

Chapter 1
Food and Your Body

Astronauts eat the foods you see in the picture during space flights. In space, foods must be easy to eat as well as healthful. You can find some foods like these in grocery stores.

The lessons in this chapter can help you choose healthful foods by giving you some information about nutrients in foods.

1 Choosing Healthful Snack Foods

2 Why Do You Need Food?

3 What Nutrients Does Your Body Need?

1 Choosing Healthful Snack Foods

Do you like to have a snack when you come home from school? Choose your snack carefully. Some foods are better than others for your body.

Look at the foods in the picture, and choose your favorites. All these foods help keep your body healthy.

Think About It

1. List your favorite snacks.
2. **Challenge** What would be good food to take with you on a long hike? Tell why you chose the foods that you did.

2 Why Do You Need Food?

Imagine you were the person who cooked the meal you see in the picture. You are proud of the food you serve. Your customers enjoy eating at your restaurant because the food tastes so good. But the taste of food is not the only reason people eat. People also eat to stay healthy.

When you eat, your body changes your food. Your teeth break the food into small pieces. Your stomach mixes your food with juices that change the food. After several hours, the food is in a form that can pass into your blood. **Nutrients** in food—substances that your body needs to live and grow—go to all the parts of your body.

nutrient (nü′trē ənt), a substance that is needed for health and growth.

Healthful foods

6

Eating healthful snacks

Your body uses some nutrients for energy. With this energy you can move your muscles and be active. Your body needs energy to repair itself when you get hurt. Nutrients give you energy for everything you do.

Other nutrients are building materials for your body. These nutrients become part of your muscles, skin, bones, and other body parts. You need nutrients to grow.

The children in the picture are eating a healthful snack. The snack will give them energy to play. The food also helps them grow.

Think About It
1. How does your body get nutrients from food?
2. Describe two ways in which your body uses nutrients.
3. **Challenge** What kind of food did you need to eat before you had teeth?

3 What Nutrients Does Your Body Need?

If you skip a meal or two, you might feel grouchy and tired. You might not have enough energy to run hard or to ride a bicycle. When you eat the foods your body needs, you have energy to play.

The six nutrients your body needs are proteins, carbohydrates, fats, vitamins, minerals, and water. Most foods cannot give you all six nutrients. You need different kinds of foods. Notice how many different foods the children are eating for lunch.

The milk provides fat, protein, a carbohydrate, some vitamins, minerals, and water. Milk is a food that gives you all six nutrients. The green salad, fruit, and beans provide other vitamins, minerals, and carbohydrates. The roll provides carbohydrates and some fats. These nutrients work together to help your body grow.

Have You Heard?

Sometimes nutrients are added to foods to make them more healthful. Breads, noodles, and rice often have vitamins and minerals added.

Lunch at school

8

Your body uses **proteins** to grow and change. Proteins also help repair injured body parts. Notice the foods, such as the meat and fish, with large amounts of proteins.

Your body uses **carbohydrates** for energy. Starches and sugars are the two main kinds of carbohydrates. Starch is the main carbohydrate in the vegetables shown. Starch is also the main carbohydrate in bread, potatoes, and rice. But sugar is the main carbohydrate in the fruits in the picture.

Your body also gets energy from **fats** that you eat. Notice which foods contain large amounts of fat, such as the olives and butter. Carbohydrates, fats, and proteins that are not used right away by your body can be made into body fat. Stored body fat can be used later for energy.

protein (prō′tēn′), a nutrient used by the body for growth and repair.

carbohydrate (kär′bō hī′drāt), a sugar or starch that is used by the body for energy.

fat, a nutrient that the body uses for energy.

Foods that contain the proteins, carbohydrates, and fats your body needs

How Do Other Nutrients Help Your Body?

vitamin (vī′tə mən), a nutrient that is needed in small amounts for normal growth and health of the body.

mineral (min′ər əl), a nutrient that helps the body work at its best.

Find Out
Look under *nutrient* in an encyclopedia to find out how much of your body is water.

You need small amounts of **vitamins** and **minerals** to keep your body working at its best. The pictures show some foods that provide the vitamins and minerals you need.

Blood is mostly water. This water carries nutrients to all parts of your body. Water also helps carry your body wastes away. You take in water in many foods and in milk and other drinks.

Think About It
1. Name the six kinds of nutrients.
2. Name some foods that provide needed amounts of each kind of nutrient.
3. **Challenge** Why would eating only one kind of food not be healthy?

Foods that provide vitamins and minerals

Do You Know?

Fiber Can Help Your Body Stay Healthy

Fiber helps keep a person healthy

Have you ever watched a chicken peck around in a farmyard? The chicken picks up feed. It also picks up bits of gravel. The chicken eats rocks!

Why would an animal eat something with no nutrients, such as gravel? Chickens and other birds need gravel because they do not have teeth. The gravel helps grind up food inside the bird's stomach. The gravel helps the bird break down its food.

You also eat things that your body cannot use as nutrients. You eat plants that are partly made of fiber.

Fiber does not get used up or changed in your body. So how can it be useful? For a long time, scientists were not sure. People who had fiber in their diets seemed less likely to get certain sicknesses. But scientists did not know why this was true.

Scientists think that fiber might soak up some chemicals that are harmful. These chemicals can cause stomach problems if the fiber is not there to get rid of the chemicals. Fiber also might soak up chemicals that cause heart problems. But the main way that fiber helps the body is by helping the body get rid of food wastes.

Fresh fruits and vegetables have a lot of fiber. Graham crackers are another food that contains much fiber. Bran—the outer coating of grains such as wheat and corn—is almost entirely made of fiber. Bran cereal, shown in the picture, is a high-fiber food.

Bran cereals are one reason you might rather be a person than a chicken. Who would want to start the day with orange juice, milk, and rocks?

Activity

Using Labels to Group Foods

Purpose
To observe food labels, and to learn which foods contain mostly proteins, carbohydrates, or fats.

You Will Need
• empty cans, jars, or boxes of foods with labels

Directions
1. Find the nutrition information on the food labels of 4 empty cans, jars, or boxes. The picture shows you where this information can be found.
2. Check to see how many grams of protein, carbohydrate, and fat there are in each food.
3. Decide whether each food is mostly protein, carbohydrate, or fat. The food in the picture is mostly carbohydrate. It has more grams of carbohydrate than of protein or fat.
4. Make a protein, a carbohydrate, and a fat group. Put foods that are mostly protein in the protein group. Put foods that are mostly carbohydrate in the carbohydrate group. Put foods that are mostly fat in the fat group.

Think About It
1. Which foods have the most of each type of nutrient?
2. Did any food have large amounts of 2 or more nutrients?
3. **Challenge** What other information can you find on the food labels?

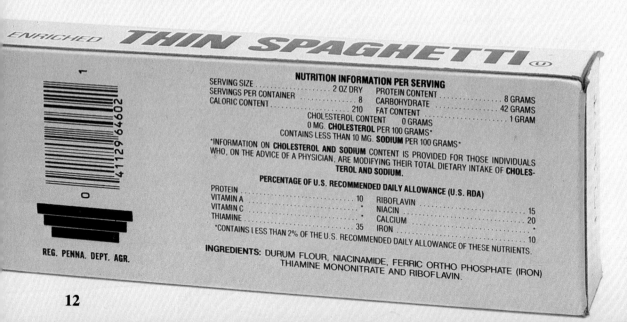

ENRICHED THIN SPAGHETTI

NUTRITION INFORMATION PER SERVING

SERVING SIZE	2 OZ DRY	PROTEIN CONTENT	8 GRAMS
SERVINGS PER CONTAINER	8	CARBOHYDRATE	42 GRAMS
CALORIC CONTENT	210	FAT CONTENT	1 GRAM

CHOLESTEROL CONTENT   0 GRAMS
0 MG. **CHOLESTEROL** PER 100 GRAMS*
CONTAINS LESS THAN 10 MG. **SODIUM** PER 100 GRAMS*

*INFORMATION ON **CHOLESTEROL AND SODIUM** CONTENT IS PROVIDED FOR THOSE INDIVIDUALS WHO, ON THE ADVICE OF A PHYSICIAN, ARE MODIFYING THEIR TOTAL DIETARY INTAKE OF **CHOLES-TEROL AND SODIUM.**

PERCENTAGE OF U.S. RECOMMENDED DAILY ALLOWANCE (U.S. RDA)

PROTEIN		RIBOFLAVIN	15
VITAMIN A	10	NIACIN	20
VITAMIN C	*	CALCIUM	*
THIAMINE	35	IRON	10

*CONTAINS LESS THAN 2% OF THE U.S. RECOMMENDED DAILY ALLOWANCE OF THESE NUTRIENTS.

INGREDIENTS: DURUM FLOUR, NIACINAMIDE, FERRIC ORTHO PHOSPHATE (IRON) THIAMINE MONONITRATE AND RIBOFLAVIN.

REG. PENNA. DEPT. AGR.

Tie It Together

Sum It Up

On a piece of paper, write the names of all the foods you might take on a picnic. List some nutrients found in each food. Describe what each nutrient does for your body.

Challenge!

1. What happens to your body if you do not get enough vitamins?

2. What nutrients are needed for making bones and teeth? What foods will provide these nutrients?

3. Why might water be considered the most important nutrient?

Science Words

carbohydrate

fat

mineral

nutrient

protein

vitamin

Chapter 2
Keeping Healthy

Weight lifting makes muscles stronger and larger. But lifting weights is only one way to strengthen muscles. Many kinds of exercise can keep your body healthy in other ways.

The lessons in this chapter describe how exercise, sleep, and cleanliness help keep you healthy.

1 Testing Your Muscle Power

Some people can hold heavy objects for a long time without getting tired. These people have strong muscles that work well.

You can test how well your muscles keep working over a period of time. Find two books about the same size. Hold one book in each hand. Stretch your arms out straight from each side, as shown in the picture. Keep this position until you cannot hold the books any longer. Write down how long you held the books. Rest, and then try again with two larger books.

Think About It

1. Did one of your arms get tired before the other one? If so, why do you think this happened?
2. **Challenge** What exercise could you do to help your arm muscles work longer?

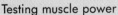
Testing muscle power

2 How Does Exercise Help Your Body?

Good food is just one of the things your body needs to stay healthy. Regular exercise is also important.

Exercises, such as those in the pictures, help you breathe more air in and out of your lungs. These exercises make your heart work harder. Then, your heart becomes stronger. The stronger your heart muscle is, the more blood your heart can pump. If your heart pumps more blood with each beat, it can beat less often. Your heart then has a longer time to rest between each beat. A strong heart might help you live longer.

Your muscles become stronger when you exercise regularly. You can use strong muscles for a long period of time. When your muscles are strong, you do not tire easily.

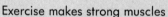
Exercise makes strong muscles

The children in the picture are doing exercises to stretch their muscles. These stretching exercises will help their muscles move smoothly.

Exercise also helps keep your body weight right for you. Your body stores extra food that is not used for energy as body fat. Exercise uses energy. When you exercise regularly, you use stored fat.

Think About It

1. How does regular exercise help your heart, lungs, and muscles?
2. **Challenge** What might happen to your muscles when you do not exercise regularly?

Have You Heard?

The strongest weight-lifters in the world can lift over 25 times their own weight. An ant doing a normal day's work, however, lifts over 50 times its own weight.

Stretching exercises

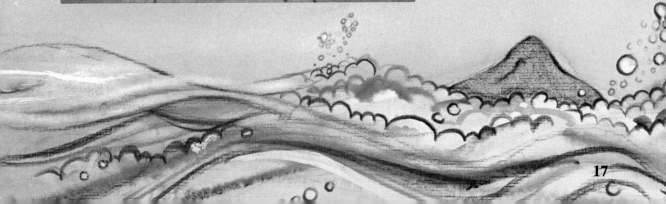

3 Why Do You Need Sleep?

If you do not get enough sleep, you might not think as clearly as usual. You might feel cranky and get angry easily.

Most eight- to eleven-year-olds need at least ten hours of sleep every night. During sleep your body gets a chance to rest, repair itself, and grow.

Notice how relaxed the sleeping girl in the picture looks. When you sleep, your muscles relax. Your heartbeat also slows, giving your heart a longer time to rest between beats.

Think About It

1. Tell three ways that sleep helps your body.
2. **Challenge** How might sleeping help you get well when you are sick?

Have You Heard?

During the deepest sleep, people's eyes move back and forth very rapidly. If a person wakes at this time, he or she will probably remember a dream.

Sleep helps your body

18

Activity

Observing Body Changes After Exercise

Purpose
To observe body changes that are caused by exercise.

You Will Need
• clock
• jump rope

Directions
1. Count how many times you breathe in 1 minute.
2. Run in place or jump rope for 3 minutes. When you finish, count how many times you breathe in 1 minute.
3. Think about which body parts you feel working as you do 10 leg lifts. The picture shows this exercise.

Think About It

1. Explain how your breathing changed after you ran or jumped. How will running or jumping help make your body stronger?
2. How did the muscles in your legs and around your stomach feel after you did leg lifts? How will this exercise change your leg and stomach muscles?
3. Which exercise was easier for you? What made that exercise easier?
4. **Challenge** What exercises could you do to help make weak muscles stronger?

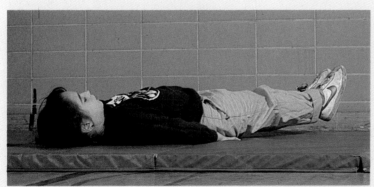
Leg lifts

4 How Can You Protect Your Skin

An orange has a skin that protects the soft, inner fruit and keeps the fruit healthy and moist. Your skin protects your body and helps keep you healthy.

Your skin covers and protects your body. Skin keeps out dirt. Your skin also helps keep your body about the same temperature in hot or cold weather.

Sometimes you need to protect your skin. Cleaning your skin helps remove the tiny **organisms**—living things—that can grow and live on your skin. Most of these organisms will not hurt you. But some organisms can cause sickness if they get inside your body. The boy in the picture is washing with soap and water. Washing removes dirt and organisms from skin.

organism
(ôr′gə niz′əm), any living thing.

Wash skin with soap and water

Too much sun can burn and damage your skin. You can protect your skin from sunburn by covering it with loose clothing. If your clothing is loose, the air can still remove sweat from your skin to keep you cool.

You are more likely to get a sunburn during the middle of the day. If you must be out in the sun, wear a lotion that blocks the sun's rays.

Protect your skin against cold weather by wearing warm clothing. The children in the picture are wearing coats, hats, gloves, and boots. Warm clothing traps heat around your body. The trapped heat keeps your skin warm.

Think About It

1. How can you protect your skin from harmful organisms?
2. How can you protect your skin from the weather?
3. **Challenge** Compare your skin with that of an animal you can observe. How is your skin different? How is it the same?

Find Out

Some people have skin that burns easily in the sun. Find out how they can protect their skin with a sun-screening lotion.

Warm clothing protects your skin

Discover!

Scientists Can Make Artificial Skin

For most of us, our skin works very well. It protects us from sickness and helps control body temperature. But artificial skin could be a big help to some people.

Artificial skin, shown in the picture, is made of two layers of materials. One layer is a rubberlike plastic. The other layer is made from the same chemicals as real skin.

When would a person need artificial skin? If a person is badly burned, much of his or her skin might be damaged. Artificial skin can help the burned surface of the body heal. Artificial skin is placed over a person's burns. The artificial skin protects the body from sickness. It covers the body until the person's skin grows back.

When the real skin has grown in place, the artificial skin falls off the body. Think how important this artificial skin could be for people who have been badly burned.

Doctor holding artificial skin

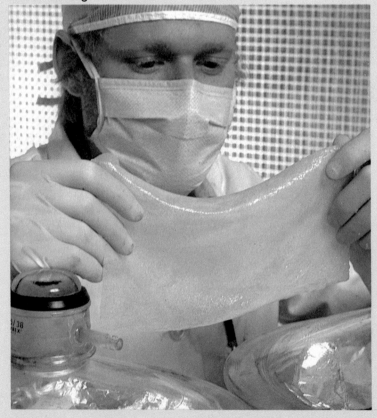

22

Tie It Together

Sum It Up

Number your paper 1–4. Look at the four pictures. Write down what the person in each picture is doing. Now, tell how each activity helps the person.

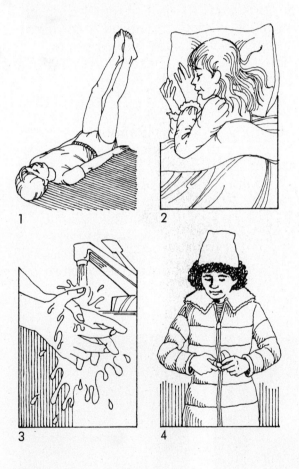

1

2

3

4

Challenge!

1. What kinds of changes might happen in the body of a person who stayed in bed for a month?

2. Suppose you saw this ad in a magazine. "Take this new pill, and forget about exercise." Do you think this statement could be true? Why or why not?

3. Suppose you have a big race tomorrow. Why do you need a good night's sleep tonight?

4. How might a tiny opening in your skin help cause sickness?

Science Word

organism

Laboratory

Starch in Foods

Purpose
To test foods for starch.

You Will Need
- waxed paper
- tape
- iodine
- medicine dropper
- several paper cups
- spoon
- cornstarch, 1 spoonful
- water
- sugar, 1 spoonful
- samples of foods, such as honey, syrup, pieces of crackers, cheese, bread, noodles, lettuce, apple, orange, potato, luncheon meat, vegetables

Stating the Problem
The starch in foods gives you lots of energy. Starch is found in many plant parts that you eat. Plants store starch in their roots and seeds. How can you test a food to see if it has starch?

Investigating the Problem
1. Tape a large piece of waxed paper onto your worktable.

2. Get a medicine dropper and several paper cups. Ask your teacher for some iodine. Put 1 drop of iodine on a corner of the waxed paper. Observe the color of the iodine. *CAUTION: Do not put the iodine near your mouth. Iodine is poisonous.*

3. Put the cornstarch in a paper cup. Add 2 spoonfuls of water to the starch. Mix the starch and water until you have a paste. See picture a.

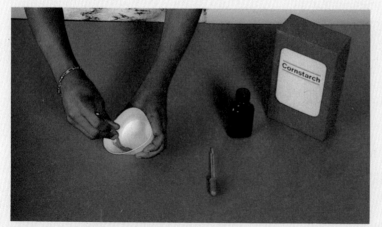

a

b

4. Put 1 drop of iodine on the starch paste. See picture *b*. Notice how the iodine changes color. Iodine changes color when it touches starch.
5. Take a second paper cup. Put a spoonful of sugar in the cup. Mix a little water with the sugar.
6. Drop 1 drop of iodine onto the sugar mixture. Watch the iodine for a color change.
7. Test other foods for starch. Test the solid foods on a clean part of the waxed paper. Test any liquid foods in a clean paper cup. For each sample of food, use 1 drop of iodine. See picture *c*.
8. Make a chart like the one in picture *d*. Write down the name of each food that you test. Make an *X* under the column *Has Starch* or under the column *Does Not Have Starch* for each food.

Making Conclusions

1. Name the foods that you tested which have starch.
2. How are the foods that have starch alike? For example, are they foods from animals or from plants?
3. Name 3 other foods that you think have starch. What makes you choose these foods?

c

Food tested	Has starch	Does Not have starch
Cornstarch		
Sugar		
Potato		
Lettuce		

d

Careers

Dancer

"Most people do not know how hard it is to be a good dancer," says Eileen. "It takes a lot of hard work and many long hours to make dancing look easy. But there is nothing I would rather do."

Eileen is a dancer and a teacher of dance. She started taking ballet lessons when she was six years old. Even though she is an adult now, she still takes lessons.

"Dancing is just like playing a musical instrument. I have to practice every day. If I am getting ready for a show, I may practice six or eight hours a day.

"Another thing I do each day is eat right. Good nutrition is very important in dancing. You need to eat right to keep your bones strong and your mind sharp. Without a good diet, it is easier to get injuries and cramps."

Eileen teaches many young people in her classes. "I think a good age to start dancing is about eight. I enjoy watching my young students learn about the world of dancing. They learn more than just how to jump high and move their bodies. My students discover that dancing is an enjoyable way to help them stay healthy."

A big part of staying healthy is eating the right kinds of foods. Many people work to make sure the food you eat is not only good-tasting, but also nutritious.

Our government has many rules about food. Foods of all kinds must pass certain tests before they can be sold at a grocery store. **Government food inspectors** check food, such as meat, to make sure it is safe to eat. They also inspect the labels on canned food to make sure the ingredients are labeled correctly.

If your school has a cafeteria, the lunch menus are probably planned by a **dietician**. The dietician is an expert in food science. This person often plans diets for people who

Food inspector

need special foods. A dietician plans nutritious meals for schools, hospitals, nursing homes, and some restaurants.

After a dietician has planned the meal, he or she may give the menu to a **cook**. The cook prepares the food. Besides restaurants, cooks work for hospitals, hotels, airlines, and schools.

Most cooks learn their skills on the job. But many people go to a cooking school. Dieticians and food inspectors learn about food science in college.

27

On Your Own

Picture Clue

Look closely at the picture on page 2. You can take a ride like this into some swimming pools.

Projects

1. Look in a cookbook to find new ways to prepare healthful foods. Choose a recipe, and ask if you can prepare a new dish for your family.

2. Keep a record of how much exercise you get for two weeks. Write down each activity that made you breathe harder and that made your heart pump faster. Record how many minutes you continued each activity.

3. Write down a dream that you can remember after you wake up. Draw a picture of your dream, or talk about your dream with your family.

Books About Science

About the Food You Eat by Seymour Simon. McGraw-Hill, 1979. Find out how cooking affects the nutrients in your foods. Learn to plan a healthy diet.

Health by Karen Jacobsen. Children's Press, 1981. How can you keep yourself healthy? This book will tell you.

Some Basics About Running by Edward Radlauer. Children's Press, 1979. Run for your health. Use this book to plan your running program.

Unit Test

Multiple Choice

Number your paper from 1–5. Next to each number, write the letter of the word or words that best complete the statement.

1. The nutrients that give you energy are
   a. vitamins.   c. minerals.
   b. carbohydrates.   d. organisms.

2. The nutrients that your body needs in small amounts to help it work at its best are
   a. proteins and carbohydrates.
   b. vitamins and minerals.
   c. fats and proteins.
   d. carbohydrates and water.

3. The body stores energy from foods as
   a. water.   c. starch.
   b. sugar.   d. fat.

4. The nutrient that helps carry the other nutrients to all parts of your body is
   a. fat.   c. water.
   b. protein.   d. energy.

5. You use energy from food to
   a. move your muscles.
   b. repair injured body parts.
   c. fight illness.
   d. Answers a, b, and c are correct.

Matching

Number your paper from 6–10. Read the description in Column I. Next to each number, write the word from Column II that best matches the description in Column I.

Column I

6. makes your muscles stronger

7. living thing

8. relaxes your muscles

9. a substance that is needed for health and growth

10. covers and protects your body

Column II

a. sleep

b. organism

c. exercise

d. skin

e. nutrient

f. sickness

UNIT TWO
LIGHT AND
SOUND

Building frames
   the other building.
Giants hanging
   over the trees.
Will they attack?
Will they fall?
Look out, little trees!

Enna Hendricks *age 8*

Chapter 3
Light Beams

Shadow tag must be played on a sunny day. The person who is "it" tags someone by stepping on his or her shadow. If you are not "it," you try to keep your shadow from getting stepped on.

The lessons in this chapter will tell you why shadows form, and what colors are in white light.

1 Seeing How Light Travels

A spotlight can help you see dancers on a stage. You can find the direction light travels from the spotlight to the stage. Get a piece of paper, a lamp, and a table. Roll the paper into the shape of a tube. Plug in the lamp, and set it on the middle of the table. Hold the tube a few centimeters from your eye. Try looking at the lamp through your tube. Can you see the light?

Use your tube to look at the lamp from different places as shown in the picture. Can you see the light from all these different places? Bend the tube downward, and try looking at the lamp. Now, can you see the light?

Think About It

1. What did you have to do to see the lamplight?
2. How does light travel?
3. **Challenge** What could you use to light the stage for a puppet show?

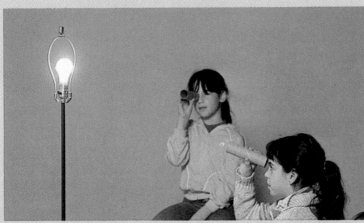

Looking at a lamp through paper tubes

33

2 How Does Light Change Directions?

You cannot read a book in a dark room. A book does not give off its own light. The girl in the picture can see her book because she has turned on a lamp. The lamp gives off light. An object that gives off light is a **source** of light. Notice that the light travels in a straight line from the source to the book. Then, it bounces from the book to the girl's eyes. When light strikes an object and bounces off, light **reflects.**

Most of the objects we see do not give off light of their own. Light from the sun, a lamp, or some other source shines on them. The objects reflect light into our eyes. The reflected light tells us what shapes, sizes, and colors the objects are.

Light reflects

34

You need a light source to see yourself. When you hold a metal tray in front of your face, light reflects off you and travels to the tray. Then, it reflects again and returns to your eyes. The boy in the picture can see an **image**—a copy of himself in the tray. The outside—or **surface**—of the tray is smooth and shiny. You can see an image of yourself when light reflects off a smooth, shiny surface.

image (im′ij), likeness or copy.

surface (sėr′fis), the outside of anything.

Think About It

1. How does light change directions?
2. When can you see an image?
3. **Challenge** Name some objects that reflect light straight back at you.

Find Out

Imagine that you want to see yourself in the mirror in a dark room. Would you shine a flashlight on your face or on the mirror?

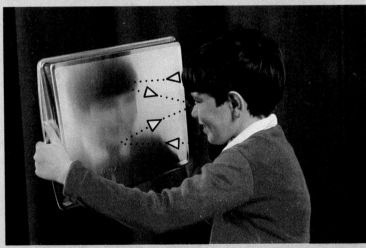

Light reflects off a smooth, shiny surface

3 What Makes a Shadow?

The pictures show how people use shadows to make a shadow theater. The object that makes the shadow is always between the shadow and the light source. An object must stop light completely to make a dark shadow.

Look at the first picture. You cannot see a shadow of the plastic wrap on the white cardboard. The plastic wrap does not stop light. The light goes through the plastic wrap because the plastic wrap is **transparent.**

In the second picture the waxed paper makes a dim shadow on the cardboard. The waxed paper is **translucent.** It stops some, but not all of the light.

transparent
(tran sper′ənt), lets light through.

translucent
(tran slü′snt), stops some light, but not enough for shadows to be seen.

Plastic wrap is transparent

The horse statue completely blocks the light. The statue is **opaque.** The dark spot on the sheet is the shadow of the horse.

A shadow theater shows you how shadows can change in size and shape. You can move the horse to make the shadow get larger and then smaller. If you move the flashlight up and down, you can see how the shape of the shadow changes.

opaque (ō pāk′), not letting light through.

Think About It

1. How do different kinds of shadows form?
2. Explain why a transparent object cannot make a shadow.
3. **Challenge** How would you move the horse to make the shadow look big and then small?

Have You Heard?
Movies make shadow pictures. The darker parts on movie films block light and make shadows on a screen.

Waxed paper is translucent

A horse statue is opaque

4 What Makes a Light Look Bright?

Imagine that you are riding in a car. Another car comes toward you. At first, the lights of the car look dim. As the car gets closer, the lights look brighter. Just before the car passes, you may turn away, because its lights look very bright.

A light seems brighter when you are closer to the source of the light. Look at the candle in each picture. The candle seems dim when you look at it from far away. As you move closer, the candle seems brighter. The candle seems to shine very brightly when you stand beside it.

The closer a light, the brighter it seems

Brightness also depends on the amount of light given off by the source. The lamps in the picture are an equal distance from you. But each lamp's bulb gives off a different amount of light. Notice which lamp looks brightest. It is the one that gives off the most light.

Think About It

1. What makes a light seem bright to you?
2. If three lights are the same distance away, how can you tell which light is brightest?
3. **Challenge** When can the brighter of two lights seem like the dimmer one to you?

Have You Heard?

Our sun is a star. It looks brighter than any other star in the sky. It only looks brighter because it is closer to earth than are the other stars.

The lamp with the brightest bulb gives off the most light

5 Where Do the Colors of the Rainbow Come From?

spectrum (spek′trəm), the band of colors formed when a beam of white light is broken up.

Most of the light we see is white light. But white light is made up of many colors. When white light shines through a drop of water, the white light breaks up into different colors. The colors you see are the **spectrum.** Red, orange, yellow, green, blue, indigo (in′də gō), and violet are the colors of the spectrum.

Sometimes you can see the colors of the spectrum when the sun shines through rain. The raindrops in the air reflect and bend the sun's white light. The sunlight is split into different colored parts, and a rainbow spreads across the sky. Notice the colors in the rainbow in the picture.

Think About It

1. What is white light made of?
2. What is the spectrum?
3. **Challenge** Where have you seen a spectrum?

Activity

Blending the Colors of the Rainbow

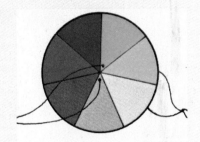

Purpose

To observe what happens when you blend the colors of the spectrum.

You Will Need

- paper circle
- piece of cardboard about 6 cm square
- paste
- crayons
- piece of string about 1 m long
- small nail

Directions

1. Color your circle like the one in the picture. Color one part of the circle violet, the next part indigo, the third part blue, the fourth part green, the fifth part yellow orange, the sixth part orange, and the seventh part red.
2. Paste the circle on the piece of cardboard, and cut the circle out.
3. With a small nail, punch 2 small holes through the dots in the circle.
4. Pass an end of the string through one hole and back through the other hole. Tie the ends of the string together as in the picture.
5. While you hold the string, ask a friend to slide the cardboard circle along the string. Keep sliding the circle until it is halfway between both ends.
6. Spin the circle around, as the girl in the picture is doing, until the string is tightly twisted. Pull gently on the ends. Keep the circle spinning at high speed by pulling and letting up on the string.

Think About It

1. As you spin the circle, what color do your eyes see?
2. **Challenge** What color would your eyes see if half of the circle were colored blue and the other half yellow?

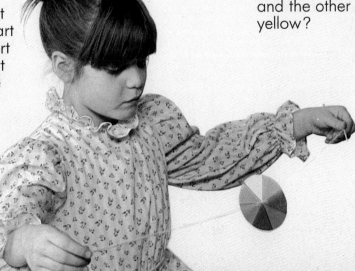

Do You Know?

How Does a Firefly Make Its Own Light?

Firefly flashing its light

Some clear summer evening, after the sun has set, you might notice tiny lights flashing in the sky. Sometimes you see these lights high above the trees. Sometimes you see them close to the ground. You might even see many lights flashing all at once in a tree, as shown in the picture. You might be surprised to learn that these lights are made by insects.

Insects that make light are called fireflies or lightning bugs. Each firefly has its own tiny taillight, as shown in the picture.

Tree full of fireflies

But a firefly cannot carry a lantern on its back! So, how does the firefly make light? Part of the firefly's tail contains two chemicals. When these chemicals mix, light is given off.

Different kinds of fireflies give off different colors of light. A firefly might give off yellow, blue, green, or red light. Different kinds of fireflies also flash their lights in different ways. Some kinds of fireflies flash once and then wait before flashing again. Other kinds of fireflies flash their lights several times in a row.

Why do fireflies flash their taillights? The flashing lights are signals to other fireflies of the same kind. By flashing its light in a certain way a firefly can find another firefly of the same kind in a tree full of different fireflies.

Tie It Together

Sum It Up

Draw a picture to go with each of these statements.

1. Light travels in a straight line.

2. You can see images when light reflects off smooth surfaces.

3. The closer you are to a light source, the more light reaches you.

4. To make a dark shadow, an object must stop light completely.

5. White light can break up into the colors of the spectrum.

Science Words

image

opaque

reflect

source

spectrum

surface

translucent

transparent

Challenge!

1. Where at school have you seen light traveling in a straight line?

2. If you were out in the sun on a hot day, how might you use a shadow?

3. How would you hold a mirror to help you see around a corner?

4. Explain why you would not be able to see a rainbow on a day when the sun is covered with clouds.

5. At what time of day would your shadow be shortest?

Chapter 4
Sound

Imagine that you are standing on the corner of this busy street. Think of all the sounds that you could hear. You might hear people talking, horns honking, engines roaring, dogs barking, or even the loud, high siren on a fire truck. All of these different sounds are alike in some ways.

The lessons in this chapter will tell you how sound travels and how music is made.

1 Making Sound

2 How Does Sound Move?

3 What Is an Echo?

4 What Makes a Sound Loud or Soft and High or Low?

1 Making Sound

Sound probably wakes you up each morning. Sound warns you of an approaching train. Sound tells you that your friend wants to play. But what is the source of sound?

Place a plastic ruler on your desk top as shown in the picture. Gently bend down the end of the ruler, and then release it. You see the ruler moving rapidly back and forth. What do you hear? When the movement stops, what happens to the sound? Slide the ruler to make the part that moves shorter and then longer. Listen carefully to the sounds you can make.

Think About It

1. What is the source of the sounds?
2. Describe ways the sounds changed.
3. **Challenge** Name some objects that make movements you can see as they make sounds.

2 How Does Sound Move?

If you throw a rock into a pool of still water, waves spread out in every direction through the water. In some ways, sound waves are like the water waves in the picture. But sound waves are invisible. And sound spreads up and down as well as out from a source.

Sounds often happen when an object moves back and forth very rapidly—or **vibrates.** Sound waves travel outward in every direction from a vibrating object. The picture shows how the sound of a school bell travels through the air.

Sound waves are strongest near the source of the sound. If you are close to the school bell, you hear it ring very loudly. As sound waves move away from the bell, they get weaker and weaker. If you are far away from the bell, you hear a very faint sound.

Waves spreading through water

vibrate (vī′brāt), move rapidly back and forth.

Sound waves spreading through air

Sound travels through many kinds of **matter**—solids, liquids, or gases. The swimmers in the picture can hear sound under water. Sound moves faster and better through water than it does through air. Sound travels best through solid matter. You can use that information to tell—or **predict**—what sounds you can hear.

In a quiet place, hold a ticking watch far enough away so you cannot hear the sound. Do you think you might hear the ticking if the sound traveled through a solid object instead of air? Before you listen, predict what you think will happen. Then put the watch at the end of a ruler or a meter stick as shown and listen.

matter (mat′ər), anything that takes up space and has weight.

predict (pri dikt′), use what you know to tell what will happen.

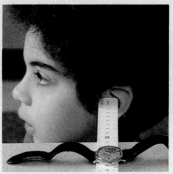
Sound waves travel through solid objects

Think About It

1. In what directions does sound travel?
2. **Challenge** Predict whether a sound would travel better through the bar of a metal fence or through air. Try it out.

Find Out

Since there is no air on the moon, how do visitors to the moon talk to each other?

Sound waves travel through water

3 What Is an Echo?

You shout "hello" near a mountain valley. A few seconds later, you hear yourself shout "hello" again. But you yelled only once!

You heard the sound bounce back. An **echo** is a sound bouncing back from an object. Sounds, like light, reflect off some surfaces. Smooth surfaces, such as some cliffs, walls, and the sides of buildings, reflect sound. In the picture the valley wall reflects sound back to the girl.

echo (ek′ō), a reflected sound you can hear.

Think About It

1. What is an echo?
2. **Challenge** Name some places where you might hear an echo.

Sound waves bounce back as an echo

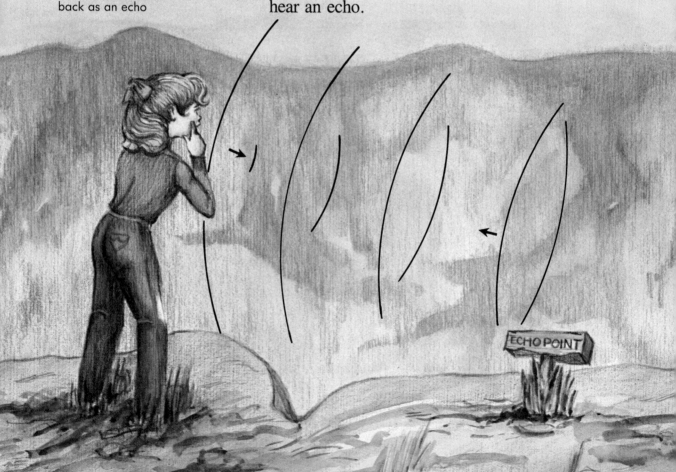

ECHO POINT

Discover!

Bats Can Observe with Their Ears

You have probably heard the saying "blind as a bat." Bats, however, are not really blind. But instead of using their eyes to observe, many bats often use their ears.

Bats that observe with their ears make high-pitched, clicking sounds. People cannot hear these high-pitched bat sounds.

Bat sounds bounce off things around the bat. The bouncing sounds make echoes that the bat can hear. The bat can tell from the echoes which kinds of objects are nearby.

When a bat flies near a wall, the bat hears one kind of echo. When the bat hears this echo, the bat changes direction to avoid flying into the wall. Bat sounds bouncing off an insect make another kind of echo. When the bat hears this echo, the bat flies toward the insect. Insects are one of the bat's main meals.

Bats usually hunt for insects and other food at night, as shown in the picture. Many bats cannot use the dim light of night to find their food. That is why these bats use sounds to "see."

People have learned from bats and other animals how to observe using sound. People have invented machines to help them observe the dark ocean depths. These machines send sound waves through the water. The sound waves echo off objects. The echoes help people steer their ships. When the sound waves hit rocks, they send one kind of echo. The machine records the echoes that tell the people where the rocks are. Then, the people can avoid the rocks.

People also use the sound-wave machines to find fish. These machines make it easier for people to catch fish. People, as well as bats, find that observing with sound is useful.

Bats observe using sound

4 What Makes a Sound Loud or Soft and High or Low?

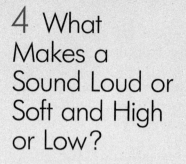

The whistles in the picture all make different sounds. Often the sounds of whistles are very loud. Sometimes whistles are soft. You may have heard someone softly whistling a tune.

Sounds can also be high or low. Some voices are very high, and some are very low. Think of people you know with high voices and those with low voices.

Stringed instruments can make loud or soft sounds. You pluck the strings with your fingers to make the strings vibrate. If you pluck the strings with great force, you hear a loud sound. Strong vibrations make loud sounds. Pluck the strings lightly, and you hear a soft sound. Weak vibrations make soft sounds.

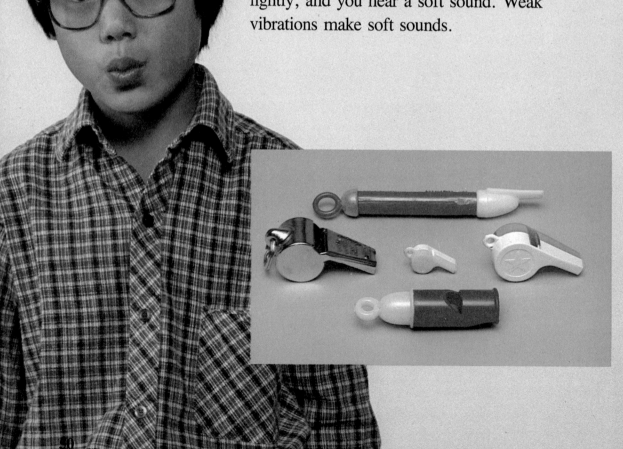

When you sing a song, your voice changes **pitch** from one note to another. Pitch means how high or low a sound is. You can change the pitch of a guitar string. If you press down on the string, as in the picture, you shorten the part that can vibrate. The shorter a string, the faster it will vibrate. Rapid vibrations make high sounds. A long guitar string vibrates slowly and makes a low sound. Slow vibrations make low sounds.

Think About It

1. What makes a sound loud or soft?
2. What makes a sound high or low?
3. **Challenge** What will happen to the pitch of a guitar string if you make the string tighter?

pitch of a sound changes in music

51

Activity

Predicting Sounds

Purpose
To predict how changing the length of the vibrating part of a rubber band changes the sound the band makes.

You Will Need
• large rubber band
• book about 24 cm long
• 2 pencils

Directions
1. Put a rubber band the long way around a book as shown. Slide the pencils under the rubber band so they are about 10 cm apart.
2. Ask a partner to hold a finger over the rubber band and each pencil, as shown in the picture. Pluck the band between the two pencils, and listen to the pitch of the sound.
3. Predict how the pitch will change if you make the vibrating part of the band longer. Record your prediction. Pluck the band when the pencils are held 19 cm apart, and listen to the pitch of the sound. Decide if your prediction was correct.
4. Predict how the pitch will change if you make the vibrating part of the band shorter. Record your prediction. Pluck the band when the pencils are held 5 cm apart, and listen to the pitch of the sound. Decide if your prediction was correct.

Think About It
1. How did the pitch change when you lengthened the vibrating part of the rubber band?
2. How did the pitch change when you shortened the vibrating part of the rubber band?
3. **Challenge** How would you use what you know to make a musical instrument?

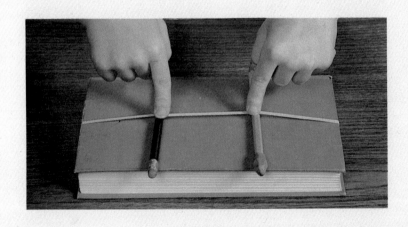

Tie It Together

Sum It Up

Unscramble the underlined words in the following paragraph. Then write the new paragraph on a piece of paper. Read the paragraph on sound.

Vibration is the rseouc of sound. Sound travels in veswa through air, water, and solid objects. Sounds can be dlou or soft, ighh or low. Pchit means how high or low a sound is. An hcoe is a sound that you hear after the sound reflects from some object.

Science Words

echo

matter

pitch

vibrate

Challenge!

1. Name a vibrating object that makes a sound you cannot hear. Is the vibration fast or slow?

2. How can you stop yourself from hearing a sound?

3. Name some places where echoes are not wanted.

4. What happens to the pitch of a sound when a record is played at too fast and then too slow a speed?

Laboratory

Musical Instruments

Purpose
To make a musical instrument.

You Will Need
• Many different materials such as rubber balloons, sandpaper, wood scraps, nails, dowels, bottles, spoons, rubber bands, bottle caps, soda straws, plastic containers

Stating the Problem
Sounds are made when something vibrates and produces sound waves. Every musical instrument has a part that vibrates. What musical instrument can you invent and make? What will your instrument need in order to make sound?

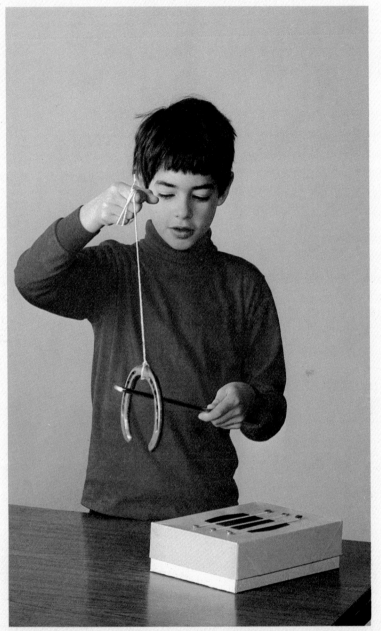

a

b

c

Investigating the Problem

1. Picture *a* shows some instruments that make sounds when they are strummed or tapped. Picture *b* shows instruments that make sounds using a flow of air. Picture *c* shows some instruments that make sounds when they are rubbed together.

2. Invent a musical instrument of your own. Make it out of the objects listed or from other objects you can get.

Making Conclusions

1. What do you need to do to make a sound with your instrument? What really makes the sound?

2. How can you change your instrument to change the pitch of the sound it makes?

3. How could you make a louder sound on your instrument?

Careers

Broadcast Technician

The lights in the television studio burn brightly as the newscaster fixes his tie. It is just a few seconds before the Evening News begins. In the control room, the director counts down, "3..2..1." A red light goes on. The director signals to the newscaster that he is on the air.

"Good evening ladies and gentlemen. Our news begins with a story about . . ."

Back in the control room, Nicole keeps a close eye on the buttons, switches, and dials in front of her. Nicole is a broadcast technician (tek nish/ən) at a television station. She is part of a crew that makes sure programs, such as newscasts, run smoothly.

"Most people do not realize all the work that goes into putting a half-hour newscast together. A crew of technicians set up and control the lights, microphones, sound recorders, cameras, and other equipment. We control much of this equipment using switches and dials in a control room."

Nicole controls the sound during a broadcast. "Before the show begins, I check the microphones that the newscasters wear. If they do not work properly, you may not be able to hear the people speak. I also check the sound level of each newscaster. Then I know how to set my dials when each newscaster speaks during the show."

But Nicole does more than just turn dials. "I have to know how all the sound equipment works. Then, if something goes wrong, I may be able to quickly correct it."

Nicole went to college for two years to learn about electrical equipment. "Some students may think I have a great job because I can meet famous people. That part of my job is interesting. But a technician should be more interested in electricity and science than in television stars."

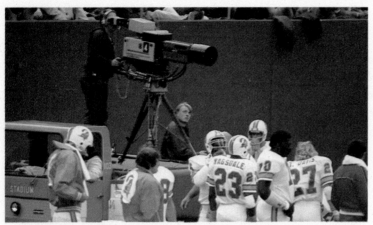
Camera operator

Photographer

Some broadcast technicians work with sound. Others work with light.

The ceiling of a television studio is usually covered with lights. A **lighting technician** controls these lights. The technician can make a studio look like it is outside on a sunny day or on a moonlit night.

The person in the studio who films a television show or movie is the **camera operator**. Some camera operators work at sports events, such as football games. What you see on the television is what the camera operator sees through the camera lens. Many cameras and camera operators are often used to film a show. This way, the audience can get different views of the same thing.

Camera operators and lighting technicians learn much of their skill on the job. But many of these workers have a good science background in high school and college.

A person who uses both lights and cameras is a **photographer**. A photographer uses lights of all kinds to make the pictures look as good as possible.

The lens in the photographer's camera is made by an **optical mechanic**. But most of the lenses this person makes are for eyeglasses. The optical mechanic cuts, grinds, and polishes the lenses to fit into the eyeglass frames.

Many photographers and optical mechanics go to special schools to learn and improve their skills.

On Your Own

Picture Clue

Look closely at the picture on page 30. Imagine that you are standing on a sidewalk, looking at the windows of a tall skyscraper. How do you know what is behind you?

Projects

1. Get a small mirror, a glass of water, and a flashlight. In a dark room, place the mirror in a glass. Let the mirror lean against the side of the glass. Shine the light through the side of the glass into the mirror. Look on the wall or ceiling to find where the spectrum is formed.

2. Write an original story with sounds. Think of the sounds you have heard on television shows. Collect some objects that make sounds. A cookie sheet is good for making thunder. Read your story to your family.

3. Make an outline of your shadow. Stand outside on a large sheet of paper in the late morning or afternoon. Ask a friend to trace your outline on the paper. Cut out the tracing, and hang it in your room.

Books About Science

Echoes by Bernice Kohn. Dandelion, 1979. Find out how sound waves bounce when making echoes.

Mirror Magic by Seymour Simon. Lothrop, Lee, & Shepard, 1981. Find out how mirrors can make light change direction.

Shadows: Here, There, and Everywhere by Ron and Nancy Goor. Crowell, 1981. Learn how you can play games with shadows.

Unit Test

Multiple Choice

Number your paper from 1–5. Next to each number,
write the letter of the word or words that best answer
the question.

1. How does light travel?
   a. in a curve
   b. in a straight line
   c. in a circle
   d. in a loop
2. What kind of surface best reflects an
   image?
   a. smooth
   b. shiny
   c. smooth and shiny
   d. rough and dull
3. Which of these objects can make a
   dark shadow?
   a. window glass
   b. plastic wrap
   c. horse statue
   d. waxed paper

4. How does distance affect the
   brightness of a light?
   a. The shorter the distance, the
      dimmer the light.
   b. The shorter the distance, the
      brighter the light.
   c. The longer the distance, the
      brighter the light.
   d. Distance does not affect
      brightness.
5. Which of these colors is in the
   spectrum?
   a. red
   b. orange
   c. green
   d. Answers a, b, and c are correct.

True or False

Number your paper from 6–10. Next to each number,
write *true* if the sentence is correct and *false* if the
sentence is incorrect. Make each false statement true by
changing the *underlined* word and writing the correct
word on your paper.

6. Sound waves are <u>weakest</u> near the
   source of a sound.
7. A <u>rainbow</u> is sunlight separated into
   colors.
8. Sound waves <u>cannot</u> travel through
   solid objects.
9. An echo is reflected <u>light</u> that
   returns to you.
10. Rapid vibrations make <u>high</u> sounds.

UNIT THREE
MAGNETISM
AND
ELECTRICITY

Chapter 5 Magnetism
Chapter 6 Electricity

Electricity
   is powerful.
And at the
   amusement park.
Your hair will
   fly up.
Shawn Mundy *age 10*

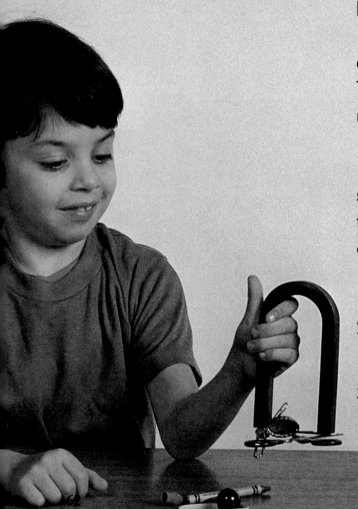

Chapter 5
Magnetism

Magnets come in many shapes and sizes. Some magnets are shaped like bars or rings. Some are shaped like horseshoes.

Small magnets can pick up only a few objects at one time. This large magnet can pick up many objects.

The lessons in this chapter will show you how you can use the force of magnetism to find directions with a compass.

1 Finding Out About Magnets

2 What Are the Properties of a Magnet's Poles?

3 Why Does a Compass Needle Point North?

1 Finding Out About Magnets

A magnet can pull certain objects toward itself. You can find out what kinds of objects a magnet will pull.

First, get a magnet, glass, rubber band, sheet of paper, pencil, pair of scissors, paper clip, thumbtack, and piece of aluminum foil. Next, hold the magnet close to each object. Make two groups. Put objects that a magnet will pull into one group. Put objects that a magnet will not pull into the other group.

Put a paper clip on a desk, and hold a sheet of paper over it as shown in the picture. Now, put a magnet against the top of the paper. What happens to the paper clip? What happens to the paper?

Think About It

1. What objects will a magnet pull toward itself?
2. What objects will a magnet not pull?
3. **Challenge** Explain what happens when you hold several pieces of paper between a magnet and a paper clip.

2 What Are the Properties of a Magnet's Poles?

If you ever spill pins on a rug, you will find that a magnet is good to have. A magnet can pick up objects with iron in them, such as steel pins.

Magnets have a **force**—a push or a pull. The force of a magnet is its **magnetism.** The magnet in the picture can pick up more pins at its ends than at its center. Magnetism is strongest at the **poles** of a magnet. The ends of a bar magnet are its poles. Most magnets have their poles at their ends.

Many bar magnets have poles marked with *N* and *S*. You can discover more about a bar magnet's poles if you let the magnet swing freely at the end of a string. When the bar magnet stops turning, the pole marked with an *N* points north. The *S* pole points in the opposite direction, which is south. Each pole of the bar magnet in the picture points either north or south.

force (fôrs), a push or pull on something.

magnetism (mag′nə tiz′əm), the push or pull of a magnet.

pole (pōl), a place on a magnet where magnetism is strongest.

Magnetism is strongest at the poles

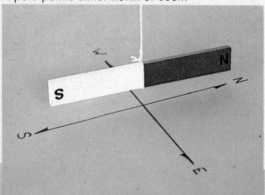
A pole points either north or south

A north pole and a south pole are opposite poles—or **unlike poles.** If you hold the unlike poles of different magnets near each other, the unlike poles pull on each other. The two magnets in the picture are pulling each other. Unlike poles pull on—or **attract**—each other.

unlike poles, poles that are opposites.

attract (ə trakt′), pull to or toward.

Unlike poles attract

What Happens When You Hold Like Poles Near Each Other?

like poles, poles that are the same.

repel (ri pel′), to push away from.

property (prop′ər tē), that which tells how a thing looks or acts.

like poles, poles that are the same.

repel (ri pel′), to push away from.

property (prop′ər tē), that which tells how a thing looks or acts.

Have You Heard?
Each half of a broken magnet will have a north pole and a south pole.

Two north poles are the same—or **like poles.** Two south poles are also like poles. The pictures show like poles from different magnets pushing each other away. Two north poles push away from—or **repel**—each other. Two south poles repel each other.

When you tell what a magnet does, you describe its **properties.** Attracting and repelling are properties of magnets.

Think About It

1. What happens when you hold like poles near each other?
2. What happens when you hold unlike poles near each other?
3. **Challenge** How can you find the poles on a horseshoe magnet or round magnet?

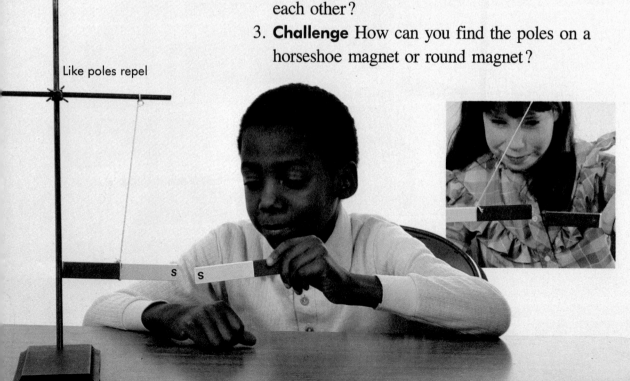

Like poles repel

Do You Know?

People Once Thought Some Rocks Were Magic

Long ago, people found certain rocks that seemed to have magical powers. The rocks, called lodestones, could make pieces of metal move. Ancient people thought that lodestones might have other powers as well. They thought that lodestones might cure sickness or help the blind to see.

But lodestones perform no such miracles. Today, we know that there is nothing really magical about a lodestone. A lodestone is simply a magnet.

All magnets attract iron. If you place a magnet near a small object that contains iron, the object will move toward the magnet. If you put a magnet on a refrigerator, the iron in the refrigerator will make the magnet stick to the refrigerator.

A piece of iron or steel can be turned into a magnet. But nothing has to be done to the iron in a lodestone to make the lodestone magnetic. Lodestones, such as the one in the picture, are natural magnets. You might say that lodestones are very attractive rocks!

Lodestones attract iron nails

3 Why Does a Compass Needle Point North?

magnetic (mag net′ik), having the properties of a magnet.

compass (kum′pəs), an object that shows directions.

The earth acts like a giant magnet. Like all magnets, the earth has **magnetic** poles. Notice where these magnetic poles are on the globe in the picture.

A **compass** helps you use the magnetic force at the earth's poles to find directions. The needle of a compass is a magnet that is free to turn. One end of the needle points to the earth's north magnetic pole. The other end points to the earth's south magnetic pole. So, you can use a compass to find the directions north and south.

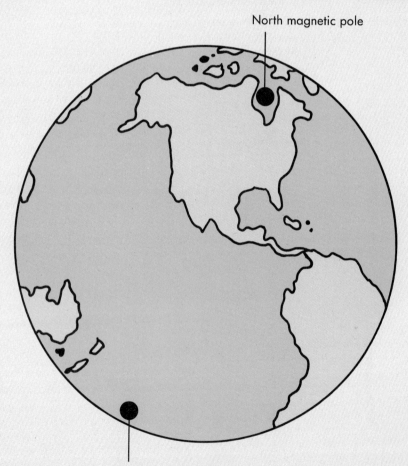

North magnetic pole

South magnetic pole

Look at the letters on the compass in the picture. The letter *N* stands for north, *S* for south, *E* for east, and *W* for west. To find directions, you move a compass until the point of the needle is over the *N*. Then, you have found the direction north. If you face north, south is to your back. East is to your right, and west is to your left.

Think About It

1. How can you use a compass to find directions?
2. **Challenge** In which directions do you walk or ride to get home from school? Use the words *north, south, east,* and *west* to explain.

Have You Heard?

Before there were compasses, ship captains needed the sun and the stars to know the direction in which they were sailing.

Find Out

Look up *compass* in an encyclopedia to find out when compasses were first used.

Compass

Activity

Making a Compass

Purpose
To make a compass, and to show how you can use it to find directions.

You Will Need
- shallow plastic dish
- small piece of wood
- clear tape or glue
- steel needle
- bar magnet
- paper
- compass

Directions
1. Half fill the dish with water. Put a sheet of paper under the dish.
2. Hold the needle by its thick end. To make your needle a magnet, rub it from one end of the magnet to the other end about 10 times. Be sure to rub the needle in the same direction each time.
3. Test the needle to see if it will pick up a pin. If not, rub the needle a few more times in the same direction.
4. Tape or glue the needle onto a small piece of wood. Place the wood in the water as in the picture. Watch the needle until it stops turning.
5. Use a compass to help you decide if your compass needle is pointing north, south, east, or west. Mark on the paper the direction the needle points.

Think About It
1. In what direction is the sharp end of the needle pointing?
2. How can you use the compass needle to find directions in the classroom?
3. **Challenge** How can you make a compass needle turn away from north?

Tie It Together

Sum It Up

Look at the pictures, and read the sentences. Number your paper from 1–4. Write the letter of the picture after the number of the sentence that explains it.

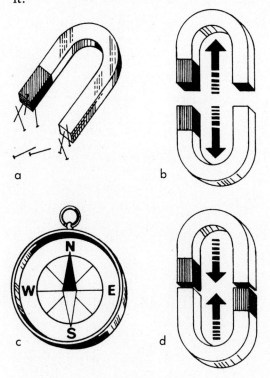

a

b

c

d

1. Magnetic force is strongest at the poles of a magnet.

2. Unlike poles of different magnets attract each other.

3. Like poles of different magnets repel each other.

4. A compass needle points north.

Challenge!

1. Name some objects through which magnetic pull cannot pass.

2. Name some toys that use magnets.

3. In what jobs might you need a compass?

Science Words

attract	magnetism
compass	pole
force	property
like poles	repel
magnetic	unlike poles

Chapter 6
Electricity

Try rubbing your shoes on a wool rug in a dark room. Then, reach out and touch a metal doorknob. If the air is dry enough, a tiny spark jumps from your hand to the metal doorknob. You feel a small shock.

The lessons in this chapter will show you how to use electricity carefully and safely.

1 Finding Out About Electricity

Sometimes objects stick together on a dry day. A wool sweater might stick to a shirt. Hair might stick to a comb or a brush.

You can make some objects stick together. Get two balloons and some wool cloth. Blow up each balloon, and tie a knot in the end. Next, rub one of the balloons against the wool cloth for half a minute. Then, hold the balloon near a friend's hair, and observe what happens.

Rub both balloons against the wool cloth. Set the balloons on a desk top 1 centimeter apart, as shown in the picture. What happens to the balloons when you take your hands away?

Think About It

1. What happens when you hold a balloon that has been rubbed against a wool cloth near dry hair?
2. **Challenge** Name some objects that are attracted to a balloon rubbed against wool.

Balloons on desk

2 How Do Charges Attract and Repel?

charge (chärj), a tiny bit of electricity.

The balloons in the picture stick to the wall. They stick to the wall as paper clips stick to a magnet. But the wall is not a magnet. What makes the wall act that way?

All matter has tiny bits of electricity called **charges.** You can not see the charges, but you can move them. When you rub two objects together, some charges might move from one object to another. A balloon rubbed against wool cloth picks up charges from the cloth. If you hold the balloon next to a wall, it sticks to the wall. The balloon and the wall have different—or unlike—charges. Unlike charges attract.

Unlike charges attract

74

If you hold two balloons with the same kind of charge near each other, they repel each other. Like charges repel.

Sometimes electric charges jump between objects with unlike charges. When charges jump from a cloud to earth, the jumping charges make sparks. The lightning in the picture is really a huge electric spark.

Think About It

1. What happens when you hold objects with unlike charges near each other?
2. What happens when you hold objects with like charges near each other?
3. **Challenge** Where have you seen electric charges acting like a magnet?

Find Out

How can you show that clothes pick up electric charges in a clothes drier?

3 How Do Electric Charges Travel?

When you turn on a flashlight, electricity makes the bulb light. To make the flashlight work, electric charges must move from one place to another. The charges travel along a path.

These pictures show how charges travel. Look at the way the bulb, battery, and wire are connected in the first picture. The charges travel along a path. They start at one end of the battery and go through the wire to the bulb. Then the charges go from the bulb back into the battery. You can tell that the path is complete because the bulb lights up.

In the second picture, you can see that the wire is not connected to the battery. The path is incomplete, so the bulb does not light.

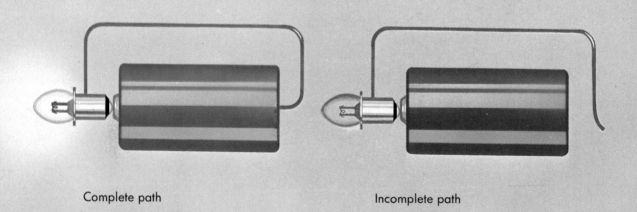

Complete path   Incomplete path

When charges travel in a complete path, they travel in a **circuit.** You can see a circuit inside the flashlight in the picture. Notice the thin wire—the **filament**—inside the bulb. As charges travel along the filament, the filament gets so hot it glows.

circuit (sėr′kit), the complete path that charges travel.

filament (fil′ə mənt), a thin wire inside a bulb.

Think About It

1. What is a circuit?
2. **Challenge** Name some toys that have circuits in them.

Have You Heard?

Electricity always travels along the shortest and easiest path that it can find.

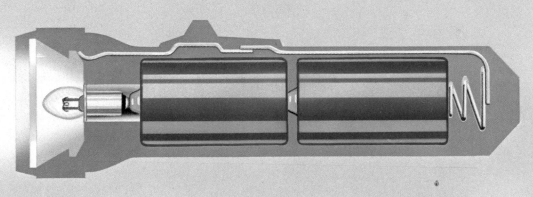

Circuit inside a flashlight

Activity

Making a Circuit

Purpose
To make an electrical circuit, and to show how it works.

You Will Need
- flashlight battery (size D)
- thin copper wire (about 30 cm) with 3 cm of covering scraped from each end
- flashlight bulb
- tape

Directions
Bend one end of the wire around the metal part of the bulb. Tape the other end of the wire to one end of the battery. Make a circuit such as the one in the picture.

Think About It
1. What happens when the bulb, battery, and wire are connected as in the picture?
2. What happens if you take the wire away from the end of the battery?
3. **Challenge** See how many other ways you can make the light shine with the battery, bulb, and wire.

Do You Know?

What Causes the Northern Lights?

Northern lights

In almost any city or town you can see signs made of flashing lights. Some of these signs use neon lights. People think of neon signs as being part of city life. But you might also see lights the color of neon signs in the night sky, high above the ground. The picture shows some of these lights called the northern lights. These lights in the sky and neon signs give off light when electric charges pass through gases.

A neon sign is made of tubes containing neon gas. Electric charges are pumped through the tubes. The tubes then give off colored light.

But what is the source of the electric charges that make the northern lights? The sun gives off electric charges that stream through space toward the earth. When the charges from the sun pass through gases in the air, colored lights appear in the sky.

These beautiful lights appear in different shapes, patterns, and colors, as shown in the picture. You might see these lights flashing in the sky on a summer night.

4 How Do We Use Electricity and Magnetism?

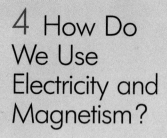

Electricity can light a lamp, cool the air, or run a motor. But you must use electricity carefully, because it can harm you.

Most of the electricity people use is made in a power station. It travels along wires from the station to your home. The wires are connected to the sockets in your home to form a circuit. Only electric plugs should be put into sockets.

Electricity moves through a lamp's circuit when you switch on the lamp. The picture shows this circuit. Never switch on any circuit when your hands are wet or when you are standing in water. You might get a dangerous shock.

Many machines use electricity to do a job. Refrigerators, washers, toasters, and many stoves, water heaters, and furnaces run on electricity.

Circuit inside a lamp

Some machines have special magnets. The magnetic forces can be turned on and off. The machine in the picture has one of these magnets. This magnet is strong enough to pick up a smashed car. Then, its magnetism can be turned off to drop the car.

The machine has a circuit with wire wound in circles—or in a coil. The coil becomes a magnet when charges flow in the circuit. The picture shows a coil picking up paper clips. The coil stops being a magnet when the electricity stops.

Any machine with a motor has a magnet that can be turned on and off. It is an **electromagnet.** Telephones and doorbells are two objects that also have electromagnets.

electromagnet
(i lek′trō mag′nit), a wire coil that becomes a magnet when electricity flows through it.

electromagnet in a junk yard

How Are Electricity and Magnetism Alike?

Like electric charges repel, just as like magnetic poles do. Unlike electric charges attract, just as unlike magnetic poles do. These properties show how electricity and magnetism are alike.

Electricity and magnetism seem to work together. The pictures show a few objects that use electromagnets.

Objects with electromagnets

Think About It

1. Name two things you should be careful about when using electricity.
2. Name five objects that use electromagnets.
3. **Challenge** Name a circuit that can be found in your home.

Tie It Together

Sum It Up

Look at these pictures. Number your paper from 1–4. Leave two spaces between the numbers. Write one or two sentences, explaining what is happening in each picture. Use these words in your sentences: charges, unlike, attract, repel, circuit, electricity, coil, magnet, safely, and socket.

1

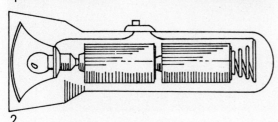

2

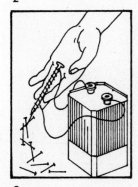

3

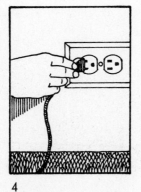

4

Challenge!

1. Name some objects that pick up charges easily.

2. How can you stop electric charges from traveling along a circuit?

3. Name some objects that were not talked about in the chapter but which use electromagnets.

4. What makes a small battery safe to use and an electric outlet dangerous?

Science Words

charge

circuit

electromagnet

filament

Laboratory

Making an Electromagnet

Purpose
To make and to observe how an electromagnet works.

You Will Need
• 1-m-long insulated, copper bell wire, with 3 cm of the insulation removed from each end
• 8-cm-long iron nail
• 3 batteries, 1.5 volts each connected end to end
• compass for showing direction
• 20 paper clips

Stating the Problem
Many machines, such as a doorbell and a telephone, use electromagnets. You can make an electromagnet and find out how it works. How could you measure the strength of your magnet? What could you do to make the magnet stronger?

Investigating the Problem
1. Wind the bell wire around an iron nail 12 times to make a small coil, as shown in picture *a*.
2. Ask a classmate to hold both ends of the wire to the batteries as shown in picture *b*.
3. Hold a compass near the coil, as shown in picture *c*. Observe what happens.

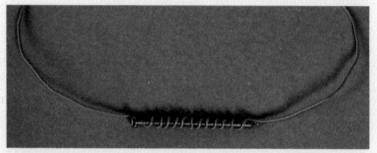

a

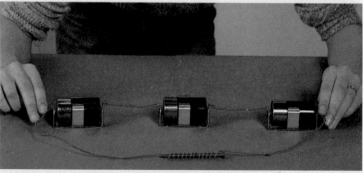

b

4. Hold the coil near a pile of 20 paper clips. Observe what happens.
5. Remove both ends of the wire from the batteries. Use the rest of the wire to make as many more turns as you can around the nail. Picture *d* shows how to do this.

6. Ask a classmate to hold both ends of the wire to the batteries once more. Hold the coil near the pile of paper clips. Observe what happens.
7. Remove one end of the wire from the batteries. Observe what happens.

Making Conclusions
1. What did your observations of the compass and paper clips tell you?
2. What happens when you make more turns in the coil of an electromagnet? How do you know?
3. How can you tell that electricity was important in making the coil act as a magnet?

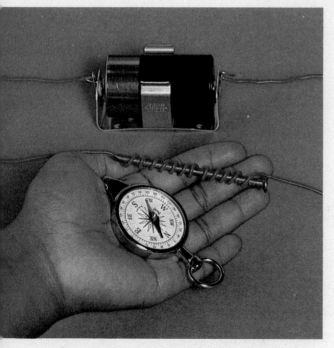
c

d

Careers

Cable Splicer

"My job takes me from underground tunnels to the tops of telephone poles," says Charlyce. She is a cable splicer with a telephone company. "My job is to install wires and make sure they go where they are supposed to go."

Charlyce works with cable, which are bundles of wires twisted together. Telephone line installers lay the cables in place. Then the splicer must connect—or splice—the wires at certain places. "Sometimes I connect the wires to telephone poles. In the city, telephone lines run underground. So I have to connect the lines underground. I connect and repair the cables mostly for office buildings and factories."

When Charlyce started working for the telephone company, she did not know much about electricity. "But I went through a lot of training on the job. I learned how to fix telephone cables and how to use electrical equipment. The company even has a class that teaches you how to climb poles! But the most important thing I learned was how to work safely around dangerous electrical equipment."

During an emergency, Charlyce may be called to work nights and holidays. "But I enjoy working with my hands. I also like helping the community."

Telephone line installer

Electrician

Without electricity, televisions, cars, refrigerators, and electric lights would not work. Many people use their knowledge and skill to make sure you get electricity.

Electricity is produced at an electric power plant. The **power plant operator** keeps the plant working.

Different operators do different things at the power plant. Some operators control the machines that produce the electricity. Other operators control the amount of electricity that flows from the plant to power lines.

Power plant operators can train on the job after high school.

When a new house is being built, you probably see carpenters and bricklayers working. But before the house is completed, you will also see an **electrician**. The electrician puts in—or installs—the electric wires in the building. The electrician makes sure all the electricity in a building works safely.

Since electricity can be dangerous, the electrician must know exactly what he or she is doing. They learn about electricity in

college. The electrician also trains on the job for a few years.

One of the most important things that works on electricity is the telephone. A **telephone line installer** installs the telephone poles and lines. When storms knock down the lines, the line installer knows how to repair the damage. Telephone line installers learn much about electricity on the job.

On Your Own

Picture Clue

Notice how the girl's hair is sticking out from her head in the picture on page 60. Something is affecting her hair. Look at the balloons sticking to the wall on page 74. Now do you know what is making her hair act that way?

Projects

1. Make a list of the ways magnets are used in the different rooms of your home. Start with the kitchen. The first example on your list might be magnets that hold notes to the refrigerator.

2. Draw and color a picture on a sheet of paper. Then, put the paper flat against a wall. Rub all parts of the picture with the side of a wooden pencil. When you take the pencil away, your picture should stick to the wall.

3. Charge a balloon and spray it all over with a small amount of water. Try sticking the balloon on a wall.

Books About Science

Look at Magnets by Rena Kirkpatrick. Raintree, 1978. Find out how electricity can change a nail into an electromagnet.

Read About Electricity by Mark W. Bailey. Raintree, 1979. Learn how electricity is made and how it gets to our homes.

Saving Electricity by Sam and Beryl Epstein. Garrard, 1977. Find out how electricity is made, and learn ways children can conserve it.

Unit Test

Matching

Number your paper from 1–5. Read the description in Column I. Next to each number, write the word from Column II that best matches the description in Column I.

Column I

1. an object that shows directions

2. the push or pull of a magnet

3. a wire coil that becomes a magnet when electricity flows through it

4. the complete path charges travel

5. can be made in a power station

Column II

a. circuit

b. electromagnet

c. magnetism

d. electricity

e. compass

f. pole

True or False

Number your paper from 6–10. Next to each number, write *true* if the sentence is correct and *false* if the sentence is incorrect. Make each false statement true by changing the underlined word and writing the correct word on your paper.

6. A magnet will attract objects with iron in them.

7. Unlike poles repel each other.

8. When you face north, east is to your back.

9. Objects with like electric charges repel each other.

10. Any machine with a motor has a special magnet that can be turned on and off.

UNIT FOUR
THE EARTH BENEATH OUR FEET

Chapter 7 Rocks and Minerals

Chapter 8 Soil

Blowing glass balls
   are colorful to see.
But sometimes
   they burst.

Charlie Lear age 10

Chapter 7
Rocks and Minerals

This mountain may not look like other mountains you have seen. It is made of marble—a kind of rock. You can see where people have been cutting away at the white marble. For years, people have used this rock to make buildings and statues.

The lessons in this chapter tell why people dig into the earth to get some minerals from rocks.

1 Naming Properties

2 What Is in a Rock?

3 What Are the Three Kinds of Rocks?

4 How Do We Mine Minerals?

1 Naming Properties

How would you describe the rock in the picture below? You might name its color and tell whether it is shiny or dull. If you could touch the rock, you might describe its weight and hardness.

Copper-colored and shiny are two properties of the rock and the penny in the picture. You can describe other objects by naming their properties.

Look at a pencil. Try to scratch the pencil tip with your fingernail. Rub the tip on a sheet of paper. List three properties of the material in the pencil tip.

Find the band around the pencil, as shown in the picture. Again, try to scratch the band with your fingernail. Rub the band on paper. List three properties of the band.

Think About It

1. Name three objects in the classroom with the same properties as the pencil's band.
2. **Challenge** Find a material with the same properties as the tip of the pencil.

2 What Is in a Rock?

mineral (min′ər əl), a material that forms from matter that was never alive.

Find Out

Collect a few different kinds of rocks from your neighborhood. Using a nail, scratch the rocks to find out which rock is softest and which rock is hardest.

While riding in a car, you may notice that the small rocks along the road all look like one color. But if you pick up one of the rocks and look closely, you may notice many colors. You might also see how bits of the rock shine in the sunlight.

Rocks are made of one or more **minerals.** A mineral forms in the earth from matter that was never alive. Minerals are different from one another because they all have their own special properties. A mineral may be any color, shiny or dull, soft or hard.

A few of the 2,500 known minerals are shown on this page. The tip of your pencil is a soft mineral called graphite (graf′īt). You can scratch the tip with your fingernail. The shiny band around your pencil is a mineral called aluminum. This mineral can be shaped into thin sheets.

Graphite

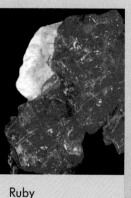

Ruby

Sulfur

Silver

The rock in the picture is granite (gran′it). Try to decide if the granite rock is made of one or more minerals.

The three minerals in the picture make up most granite. Quartz (kwôrts) is a hard mineral. It is often shiny and white, but may be tan, purple, or yellow. Tan-colored sand is mainly tiny pieces of quartz.

Feldspar (feld′spär′) can be white, pink, red, green, or blue. When feldspar breaks into fine, tiny pieces, it becomes clay.

Mica (mī′kə) is a soft mineral that forms in shiny, thin layers. Mica can be black, gray, or grayish white.

Try to point out the quartz, feldspar, and mica in the granite.

Think About It

1. What is a mineral?
2. **Challenge** A pearl is made inside an oyster. Is a pearl a mineral? Why?

Have You Heard?

Over one hundred years ago, people made false teeth from white feldspar. They made windows from thin sheets of clear mica.

Granite

Quartz

Feldspar

Mica

3 What Are the Three Kinds of Rocks?

igneous (ig′nē əs) **rock,** rock that forms from melted minerals.

If you have a stamp collection, you might group the stamps by countries. How would you group rocks in a rock collection? You could sort the rocks by color, but some rocks have many colors. First you must decide how you will group the rocks in your collection. Then you can sort them.

Deep inside, the earth is so hot that minerals melt. When the melted minerals rise toward the surface, they cool and harden into rock. Rock that forms from melted minerals is **igneous rock.** Granite is an igneous rock.

Sometimes, at a volcano, melted minerals ooze out onto the earth's surface. These melted minerals cool and form igneous rock like that in the picture.

Igneous rock

Most of the rocks that people see were once under lakes and oceans. Over the years, rivers carry bits of rock, plants, shells, and bones into lakes and oceans. The bits of rock and other materials sink to the bottom of the water as **sediment.**

Over many years, layers of sediment collect on the lake or ocean floor. The weight of the top layers presses the lower layers into **sedimentary rock.** The picture shows many layers of sedimentary rock. The layers look different because they have different kinds or sizes of sediment. These layers were once under a body of water.

sediment (sed′ə mənt), bits of rock and other material that sink to the bottom of a river, lake, or ocean.

sedimentary (sed′ə men′tər ē) **rock,** rock that forms from sediment being pressed together.

Sedimentary rock

metamorphic
(met′ə môr′fik) **rock,**
igneous or sedimentary
rock whose minerals have
been changed by heat and
pressure.

Igneous or sedimentary rock can change to form **metamorphic rock**—the third kind of rock. Strong heat inside the earth may change a rock's minerals into other minerals. The pressing of rocks can also change minerals. When the minerals change, the rock becomes a metamorphic rock.

Limestone is a common sedimentary rock. When limestone is heated and squeezed inside the earth, the limestone becomes marble, as shown. Marble is a metamorphic rock.

Think About It

1. List the three kinds of rock, and explain how each kind forms.
2. **Challenge** Explain how an igneous rock can become part of a sedimentary rock.

Metamorphic rock: marble

Activity

Identifying a Rock

Purpose
To describe a rock so someone can identify it.

You Will Need
• 5 rocks for each group
• sheet of paper
• masking tape
• felt-tip pen

Directions
1. Work in groups of 4 people. With a partner, choose 5 rocks from your teacher's collection.
2. Use the masking tape and pen to number each rock as shown in the picture.
3. Choose one of your numbered rocks. Study the rock. Observe and record its size, color, shape, and whether it is smooth or rough. Be sure the other two members of your group cannot see which rock you choose.
4. Bring the 5 rocks to the other two members of your group. Place the rocks on a sheet of paper.
5. With your partner, describe the rock you chose to the other two members of your group. Ask them to identify the rock and to tell you its number.
6. Let the other two members of your group pick 5 rocks and repeat the activity.

Think About It
1. What did you say about your rock to help other people identify it?
2. **Challenge** Name another way to describe a rock besides those listed in step 3.

4 How Do We Mine Minerals?

ore (ôr), rock that contains enough of a useful mineral to make it worth mining.

Find Out

Use an encyclopedia or look around your house to find 3 uses of copper and 3 uses of iron.

How often have you used minerals today? Did you get food from a refrigerator? Did you ride your bicycle to school? Have you stapled any papers? Refrigerators, bicycles, and staples are made from minerals.

Before people can use minerals, they must find them and take them from rock. People look for rock that contains large amounts of a mineral. If the mineral can be sold for more than the cost to get it, the rock is valuable. Valuable rock is called an **ore.**

Copper ore is a rock with the mineral copper in it. Iron ore is a rock with the mineral iron in it. The mineral must be separated from the rest of the rock.

Open pit copper mine

Sometimes minerals are deep underground. In order to get the minerals, we must dig deep tunnels—or shafts—as in the drawing.

Often, the minerals are near the earth's surface. Miners remove the soil and top layers of rock to reach the ore. Land must be removed over a large area. As you can see, this kind of mining leaves a large pit in the ground. But in many states, mining companies must fill in the pit and make the land usable again. Some parks are built over filled-in mines.

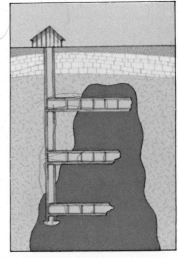

Underground mine

Think About It

1. What is an ore?
2. Explain two ways people mine ore.
3. **Challenge** Why do you think most minerals are mined only where they are found in large amounts?

Do You Know?

How Does Rock Become Part of a Bicycle Wheel?

Factory worker shapes bicycle wheel

Iron, aluminum, and chromium are three metals used in making bicycles. These metals all come from mineral ores. When the metals are first dug out of the ground, they look very different from metals you usually see.

Many things must be done to remove the metal from rock that contains the mineral ore. First, the ore is dug from the ground. Next, the ore is separated from soil and rocks. Then, the metal is removed from the ore.

Sometimes, heating the ore removes the metal from the rest of the rock. Other times, chemicals must be added to help separate the metal from the ore. Electricity might also be used to remove the metal from ore.

In the next step the metal is made into special shapes. Chromium, for example, is formed into sheets, wire, or rods, or is made into a powder.

Finally, the metal goes to the bicycle factory. The picture shows a person cutting and shaping the metal to make a bicycle wheel. The dirtlike ore, dug from the ground, has become part of a bicycle!

Tie It Together

Sum It Up

Number a sheet of paper from 1–10. Next to each number, write the word or words from the list below that fit the description by that number.

feldspar   metamorphic rock
granite   mineral
graphite   ore
igneous rock   sediment
marble   sedimentary rock

1. I am found in all rocks. I am made from matter that was never alive.

2. I am a soft mineral that you can find at the tip of your pencil.

3. When I break into tiny pieces, I become clay.

4. I am a rock that forms when melted minerals harden.

5. I am an igneous rock made from quartz, feldspar, and mica.

6. I sink to the bottom of water and make layers.

7. Layers of sediment press together to make me.

8. Under heat and pressure, I change from one kind of rock to another.

9. I used to be limestone. People sometimes use me to carve statues.

10. Miners dig me up because people use my minerals.

Challenge!

1. Coal is made from dead organisms. Is coal a mineral? Why?

2. Explain how a metamorphic rock could become part of an igneous rock.

3. The sedimentary rocks that you see were once under lakes or oceans. What might have happened in order for you to see these rocks today?

4. Name two minerals that might be mined even if there are not a lot of those minerals in that place.

5. Name some foods that are formed like igneous, sedimentary, or metamorphic rock.

Science Words

igneous rock

metamorphic rock

mineral

ore

sediment

sedimentary rock

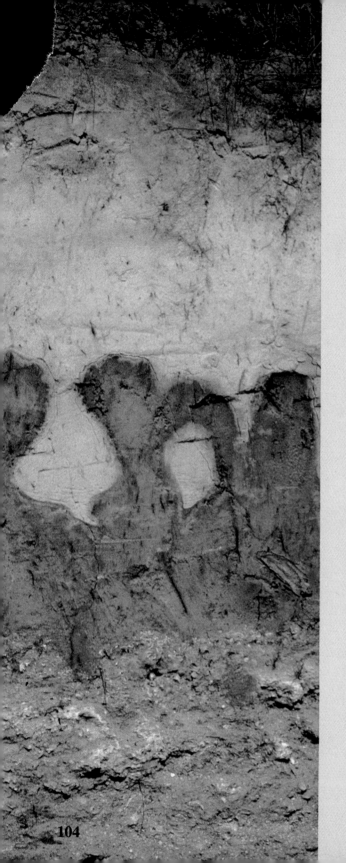

Chapter 8
Soil

You may think of soil as just something you wash off after playing outside. But soil does a lot more than get you dirty. People use soil to grow food.

The picture shows what some soil looks like under the blanket of grass. Certain minerals in the soil give soil its different colors.

The lessons in this chapter tell how soils are different and why plants grow better in certain kinds of soil.

1 Examining Soil

2 Where Does Soil Come From?

3 How Are Soils Different?

1 Examining Soil

Look at the pictures of plants growing in different soils. Do different kinds of soil affect the way plants will grow?

Ask your teacher for three separate cups of soil. Place a little bit of soil from each cup on a sheet of paper. Describe the color of each kind of soil. Is the soil loose or tightly packed?

Plant the same kind of seeds in each of the three cups of soil. Keep the seeds watered and in a sunny spot. Over two weeks, observe how well the plants grow.

Think About It

1. How are the soils in the cups different?
2. **Challenge** What properties of the soils do you think helped your plants grow best?

Plants growing in different soils

2 Where Does Soil Come From?

The boulder in the picture is very big. You would need a machine to move it. But over thousands of years, the boulder will slowly crumble and become part of the soil!

Soil is a mixture of crushed rock, once-living matter, air, and water. Look at the pictures. As the rocks were broken, the pieces got smaller and smaller. In the last picture the pieces of rock are so small, they are called sand grains. The next time you dig in the soil, check for sand and other pieces of rock.

Rocks break apart and form soil

But how can large, solid rocks break into pieces? The drawing shows one way that rocks break apart. If you look closely at a boulder, you will see many tiny holes and cracks. Water from rain or snow fills the holes and cracks. When the water freezes, it takes up more space. The freezing water pushes against the rock, as the arrows show. As melting and freezing continue, the rock slowly breaks apart.

Freezing water breaks rock

How Do Living Things Help Make Soil?

The plant in the picture is breaking the rock apart. Soil collects in the cracks. Plants can grow in this soil. As each plant grows, roots push against the rock and break it. Over the years, roots of plants can help crumble a large rock.

Besides rock, soil has air, water, and matter that was once alive. When plants and animals die, they rot—or **decay.** As the dead plants or animals decay, they become part of the soil. This decayed matter—or **humus**—gives soil its dark color. Humus adds nutrients to the soil which plants need to grow.

Have You Heard?

Very slowly, worms and other animals scrape off tiny pieces of rock as they crawl or walk over them.

Think About It

1. What is in soil?
2. How can water crack rocks?
3. **Challenge** What might happen to a sidewalk that has a large tree growing near it?

Plants help to break rock

Do You Know?

Soil Can Be a Clue to a Mystery

Police use a microscope to look for clues in soil

A police detective walks into the room where a crime took place. Every part of the room will be searched for clues. The doorknobs and furniture will be closely looked at for fingerprints. Detectives will look for threads or bits of cloth that might have been torn from the criminal's clothes. But the best clue in this crime might turn out to be dirt!

Police use science to give them information about crimes. The police will put soil found on a suspected criminal's shoes under a microscope, as shown in the picture. What does the detective expect to find?

Soils that come from different places are not the same. The soils have different amounts of sand and clay. Soils also contain different types and amounts of minerals. By looking at the soil through a microscope, the detective can find out exactly what the soil is made of.

Then, the detective will use a microscope to look at soil found in the room where the crime took place. If the soil from the suspect's shoe and the soil from the room where the crime took place are exactly the same, the detective will know that the shoe had been in that room. And since the shoe belongs to the suspect, the suspect might have been there too.

The soil could be an important clue to help the police solve the crime. Without knowledge of soils, the soil on the suspect's shoe and the soil in the room would simply be dirt.

3 How Are Soils Different?

Soil in your lawn or neighborhood park is different from soil in other parts of the country. Soil comes in many colors. It can be as soft as cotton or as hard as a brick.

The girl is holding soil that has a lot of humus. Notice how this soil is dark brown or black. Soil might be other colors, depending on the rock that formed the soil. Iron in the rock makes soil red, brown, or yellow.

Look carefully at the soil grains in the pictures. Each grain of the clay soil is very tiny. The small size of the grains makes clay feel smooth.

The grains of the sandy soil are larger than clay. Sandy soil is loose and easy to dig.

In order to be good for planting crops, soil must have air and water. Air and water fill the spaces between soil grains.

Clay soil

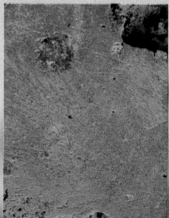

Sandy soil

Clay holds water. But the grains are packed too tightly to allow plants to grow well. Sand is loose, but it does not hold much water.

Good planting soil is a mixture of sand, clay, and humus. This soil is easy to dig, holds water, and has nutrients for plants. If soil does not have enough humus, some farmers might add nutrients—fertilizer—as shown in the picture.

Think About It

1. What makes some soils red?
2. Describe a good planting soil.
3. **Challenge** How do you think sandy soil would feel to your skin if you rubbed it against your hands.

Farmer adding fertilizer to a field

Activity

Testing How Much Water Soil Holds

Purpose
To test the amount of water that soils hold.

You Will Need
- potting soil
- sand
- dry clay
- 4 large baby-food jars with covers
- strainer or piece of cloth
- small pan
- water
- hand lens
- centimeter ruler

Directions
1. Examine the 3 kinds of soil with the hand lens.
2. Fill three jars a little less than halfway with a different kind of soil.
3. Half fill the fourth jar with water. Pour that amount into each jar of soil.
4. Put the covers tightly on the 3 jars, and shake them.
5. Take the cap off 1 jar. Cover the jar with a strainer or cloth, and hold it over the pan.
6. Carefully pour the soil and water into the strainer or onto the cloth, as shown. Let the extra water drain into the pan. Do not squeeze any water out of the soil.
7. Pour the water from the pan into the last jar. Using the ruler, measure and record the amount of water. Then empty the jar.
8. Repeat steps 5–7 for the other 2 jars.

Think About It

1. Which soil held the most water? How do you know?
2. Which soil held the least water? How do you know?
3. **Challenge** How did some soils hold more water than others?

112

Tie It Together

Sum It Up

Read the imaginary conversation between a plant, a large rock, and soil. Number your paper from 1–10. Next to each number, write the name of the object you think is saying that sentence or group of sentences.

1. "How can you grow on me? I thought plants grew in soil."

2. "They do. You have soil in your cracks."

3. "I got a lot of new cracks last winter from freezing water."

4. "My growing roots will push against you. Over many years a lot of us can help break you apart."

5. "What will happen to me then?"

6. "Part of you might become more like me, as you break into tiny pieces."

7. "Do you mean I might become part of the soil?"

8. "Yes. In fact, I have a lot of rock pieces in me right now."

9. "So, you came from things like me and this plant?"

10. "Right. When people pick me up, they may be picking up parts of a boulder and a tree!"

Challenge!

1. Describe what the first few centimeters of good planting soil might look like.

2. Would a boulder become part of the soil in your lifetime? Explain.

3. After a rainstorm, what would dry faster, a sandy beach or a field with a lot of different plants? Why?

4. What makes sandy soil feel different from clay soil?

Science Words

decay

humus

Laboratory

Mineral Hardness

Purpose
To compare the hardness of different minerals.

You Will Need
- graphite pencil
- penny
- samples of the minerals quartz, feldspar, and mica

Stating the Problem
Would a statue made of quartz be harder and last longer than a statue made of feldspar or mica? What do you need to know about these minerals to decide which mineral would be best to use when making a statue?

Investigating the Problem
1. Hard minerals will make a scratch on softer minerals. A penny is harder than the mineral graphite in a pencil. Use a penny to scratch the graphite of a pencil, as shown in picture a. Observe what happens.

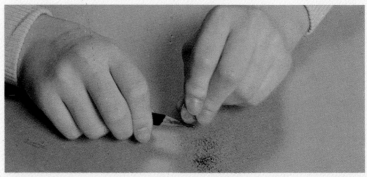

a

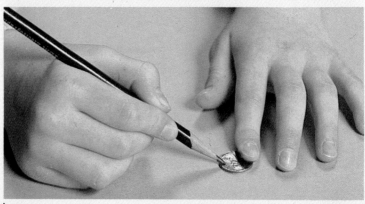

b

2. Now, scratch the penny with the graphite, as shown in picture *b.* Observe what happens.
3. Use samples of the minerals quartz, mica, and feldspar to learn which mineral is the hardest.

Observe which mineral will scratch which other mineral, as shown in picture *c.*
4. Copy the chart into your notebook. Fill in the chart with your observations.

Mineral	Other minerals it scratches
1. quartz	
2. mica	
3. feldspar	

Making Conclusions
1. List the minerals quartz, mica, and feldspar in order from the softest to the hardest.
2. Which mineral would be best for making a statue? Why?
3. The mineral talc is softer than mica. Will talc scratch quartz?

c

Careers

Salt-Mine Manager

If everything goes well, Jack's mine will produce 1,500,000 tons of salt this year! Jack is the manager of a salt mine in Louisiana.

"There are three ways to get salt," says Jack, "brining, mining, and sunshining. In brining, we drill down to where the salt is. Then, we force fresh water down into the salt. The water mixes with the salt to make a brine—or very salty water. We pump it up and boil it. The water evaporates and leaves very fine salt crystals. This is the salt you put in your salt shaker.

"In salt mining, we dig down to the salt deep in the earth.

"Sunshining is another way to get salt. We put salt water from the ocean into large ponds. The sun

evaporates the water and the salt settles to the bottom of the pond."

Jack began working for the salt company when he was at college in Utah. Now, he is in charge of a salt mine and a salt plant. The plant is where the salt is prepared for use.

"The company I work for has mines and plants all over North America. They produce about 300 different kinds of salt for people and animals."

Salt is often used at the dinner table. But farmers also give salt to their animals to keep them healthy. People use salt to melt ice on streets. Salt is used in the building of roads. "But most of the salt we mine is used to make chemicals. Without the chemicals made from salt, we could not produce paper, soap, glass, and other products."

Many of the things you use come from rocks and minerals. Certain rocks and minerals may be needed to make toys, bicycles, and buildings.

A quarry is a large pit where slabs of rock are taken from the earth. This rock is used for buildings, bridges, and dams. **Quarry workers** cut and haul out the rock. They use many tools including picks, crowbars, special saws, and huge cranes. Quarry workers learn their skills on the job.

Many minerals are gems used as jewelry. But gems, such as diamonds and rubies, do not become beautiful jewels until a **gem cutter** cuts and polishes them. The gem cutter carefully studies the uncut gemstone. Then, he or she knows exactly how to cut the gem. If it is not cut correctly, it may shatter.

A person who wants to be a gem cutter can learn the skills on the job. Some gem cutters take special classes after high school.

The thousands of different minerals come in many shapes, sizes, and colors. If you enjoy collecting and observing minerals, you might like to be a **mineralogist** (min′ ə-rol′ ə jist). This person studies minerals. He or she can tell where different minerals may be found and how they can be useful to people. If you think you might like this career, you should learn more about minerals and study science in college.

Gem cutter

Quarry worker

On Your Own

Picture Clue

The glob at the end of the rod on page 90 is made of minerals. When this object is formed and cooled, it will be very hard. If dropped, it could break into sharp pieces.

Projects

1. Start your own rock collection. Find a few rocks when you are on vacation or walking around your neighborhood. Label your rocks with information about the part of the country where you found them, and about whether they were found near water or in a dry area. You might sort your rocks by color, by hardness (scratch them with a fingernail or a penny), or by where they were found.

2. Talk with a soil scientist, or visit a farm. Find out what type of soil is in your area and what crops usually grow best there. Ask farm managers if they add anything to their soil to help their crops grow.

3. Make a rock garden in a plastic or a clay container. Choose a sandy soil or one with a lot of humus. Find a plant that grows in the soil you chose. Make patterns in your garden with pieces of rock or colored glass.

Books About Science

Beneath Your Feet by Seymour Simon. Walker, 1977. This book will make you think about what you are walking on outside. It tells you how soils form and how they are different.

From Sand to Glass by Ali Mitgutsch. Carolrhoda Books Inc., 1981. This book tells about melting sand and mixing it with soda, lime, and recycled glass to make new glass products. See also *From Clay to Bricks* and *From Ore to Spoon*.

How to Dig a Hole to the Other Side of the World by Faith McNulty. Harper and Row, 1979. This book takes you on a fantasy adventure, but it tells facts about the inside of the earth.

Unit Test

Matching

Number your paper from 1–5. Read the description in Column I. Next to each number, write the word or words from Column II that best match the description in Column I.

Column I

1. rock formed from melted minerals
2. bits of matter that sink to the bottom of bodies of water
3. rock changed under heat and pressure
4. decayed plant and animal matter
5. rock formed from bits of matter pressed together in layers

Column II

a. metamorphic rock

b. minerals

c. humus

d. sediment

e. sedimentary rock

f. igneous rock

Multiple Choice

Number your paper from 6–10. Next to each number, write the letter of the words that best complete the statement.

6. Minerals are
   a. plant and animal matter.
   b. matter that was never alive.
   c. only found in sedimentary rock.
   d. formed from decayed plants.

7. Ore is
   a. a kind of rock.
   b. a valuable substance.
   c. dug from a mine.
   d. Answers a, b, and c are correct.

8. Rock is
   a. always the same hardness.
   b. made of decayed animal matter.
   c. never changed.
   d. made of minerals.

9. Soil contains
   a. air and water.
   b. living things.
   c. decayed plant and animal matter.
   d. Answers a, b, and c are correct.

10. Humus helps plants grow because
    a. it does not hold water.
    b. it adds nutrients to soil.
    c. it comes from igneous rock.
    d. it makes soil light colored.

UNIT FIVE
FOSSILS

Insect.
Held inside a golden pool.
Struggling to get out
   and live.
The pool hardens;
   it is a trap.

Adrienne Freed *age 10*

Chapter 9
Life from the Past

Sometimes a beach is totally covered with beautiful shells. Some are picked up by people and taken home. Many shells crumble and become part of the sand. A few shells might be buried. Far into the future, someone might uncover the buried shells.

The lessons in this chapter tell about some of the best places to find fossils.

1 Observing and Deciding

2 What Are Fossils?

3 Where Can You Find Fossils?

1 Observing and Deciding

Suppose you looked out your window in the morning and saw water on the driveway. Maybe it rained during the night. Maybe someone was washing a car or watering flowers. If every place outside were wet, it probably had rained.

You often observe the present (water everywhere) to decide what you think happened in the past (it rained). Observe the kitchen floor in the picture. Decide what happened in the past.

You can practice observing things and deciding with your classmates. On a sheet of paper, trace around an object in the classroom. You may choose a small book, a jar lid, or even your hand. Now, cut the paper into fourths. Show one piece at a time to a classmate. Each time, ask the person if he or she can decide what the object is.

Think About It

1. Suppose you saw someone walking near a lake, carrying a lot of fish. Decide what you think the person had been doing.
2. **Challenge** In the picture, how could you tell which way the person with the muddy shoes had been moving?

2 What Are Fossils?

evidence (ev′ə dəns), clues that give information.

fossil (fos′əl), sign or evidence of past life.

preserve (pri zėrv′), keep from decaying.

Have You Heard?

Oil, coal, and natural gas form over millions of years from organisms.

In many mystery stories the clever detective observes clues—or **evidence**—to solve crimes. Scientists also observe evidence. Scientists usually do not solve crimes, but they do make exciting discoveries!

A **fossil** is a sign or evidence of past life. Some fossils may be millions of years old. A fossil may be a bone, a tooth, or a whole plant or animal. Tracks of a plant or animal are also fossils. Many clues to the past are in fossils.

One way organisms become fossils is by freezing. If you have a freezer at home, you know that food does not decay in the freezer. Food, such as hamburger and celery, will decay in a room. Over time, some food even spoils in the refrigerator. But freezing **preserves** food by greatly slowing the decay.

Freezing can also preserve whole organisms. The picture shows a woolly mammoth found frozen in Siberia. Although the mammoth died about ten thousand years ago, it has not decayed.

Woolly mammoth

Look at the picture of the insect. The insect became trapped in the sap of a tree. The yellow sap hardened and preserved the insect. This kind of fossil is unusual. Even the thinnest parts of the organism are preserved.

Some fossils formed when animals were buried in tar. Pools of sticky tar formed from oil that oozed above the ground. Animals often fell into the tar and could not get out, as the drawing shows. The bones and teeth of these animals were preserved in the tar.

Insect trapped in amber

125

What Are Other Ways Fossils Form?

Organisms are preserved in ice, in tar, and in hardened tree sap. And some fossils are organisms that turned slowly into stone!

The picture shows a forest in Arizona that became **petrified**—or turned into stone. Scientists think these trees fell millions of years ago. Sediment slowly covered the trees. As time passed, water trickled down to the buried trees. Minerals mixed with the water as it trickled through the soil. Bit by bit, the wood was replaced by minerals. The trees slowly became logs of stone!

petrify (pet′rə fī), turn into stone.

Petrified wood

Most fossils come from sea organisms. Suppose a shellfish, such as a clam, dies and falls to the sea floor. Over time, sediment in the sea sinks to the bottom and covers the shell. The shell may decay. But the sediment hardens into rock, leaving a print of the shell. The print is a **mold.** Minerals in water may fill the mold. The minerals harden and make a **cast** of the shell. The picture shows a cast of an organism that died long ago in a sea.

mold (mōld), a print left in a rock by a decayed organism.

cast (kast), shape of an organism that is made by filling a hollow space.

Most fossils are molds or casts. You can compare a fossil mold and cast to that of the gelatin dessert shown in the picture.

Think About It

1. What is a fossil?
2. Explain two ways that fossils form.
3. **Challenge** Do you think all dead organisms become fossils? Why?

Fossil cast

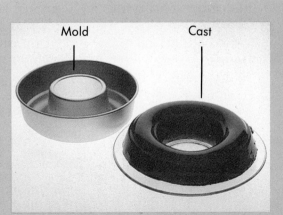

Mold   Cast

Activity

Preserving Plant Parts

Purpose
To observe the results of different ways of preserving plant parts.

You Will Need
• 5 leaves or petals
• plastic wrap
• dry soil (sand, clay, or potting soil)

Directions
1. Copy the chart shown here on a piece of paper.
2. Use 4 ways to try to preserve your leaf or petal. You might use the following ways: 1) place it between the pages of a book; 2) wrap it in plastic wrap; 3) place it in a freezer or refrigerator; 4) cover it with dry soil.
3. Fill in the first 2 columns of the chart.
4. Store your plant parts in the 4 ways for 7 days. Keep the fifth plant part out in the open in the classroom.
5. After 7 days, collect and observe your plant parts. Compare their color, stiffness, and anything else you observe.
6. Fill in the third column of the chart.

Think About It
1. What way or method worked best to preserve the plant parts?
2. Compare the plant part left in the open with the other plant parts.
3. **Challenge** Why do people put meat in a refrigerator or freezer?

What I am preserving: _____

How I will preserve it	How object looked before I preserved it	How object looked seven days later

Do You Know?

Some Buildings Contain Fossils

Buildings made of limestone or marble might contain fossils. You might find fossils in rock cut to make space for new houses. When a road is cut through a hill of rock, fossils can sometimes be found.

Broken pieces of rock and stone that you find on the ground might contain fossils. You might also find fossils if you walk along a stream, a river, a lake, or an ocean.

If you go fossil hunting, like the people in the picture, watch for shapes that look like pieces of plants, animals, or shells. These shapes were formed from animals or plants that once were alive. You might even find the shape of an animal's footprint as a fossil. But you probably will not find many complete fossils. They get broken in the earth over time.

What can you do if you find fossils, such as those in the picture? First, record the place where you found your fossils. Then, find out the names of your fossils. You might find a book which will help you label the fossils that you find.

In some parts of the country, fossils are very common. If you observe carefully, you might find fossils that can help you learn how some animals and plants might have looked years ago.

Fossil hunting

Fossil shells

3 Where Can You Find Fossils?

Fossil crinoid stem

You may want to go on a fossil hunt to learn more about fossils. Where do you start?

The best place to look for fossils is in sedimentary rock, especially limestone. You can probably find sedimentary rock around your city or area. You often see this kind of rock along a river or road, as shown.

In your search for fossils, do not expect to find a skull or other large bones. Most fossils will be the remains of shells or small, hard parts of other sea creatures. The small fossil in the picture may be millions of years old. This fossil came from the long, skinny part of the organism in the drawing.

Think About It

1. Where is the best place to find fossils?
2. **Challenge** Why do you think full skeletons of large animals are not often found as fossils?

Sedimentary rock: limestone

Tie It Together

Sum It Up

Number your paper from 1–8. Choose a word from the list that will help complete each sentence. Write the word on your paper beside the number of the sentence. Use each word only once.

tar	sedimentary
fossils	sea
small	insects
petrified	molds
frozen	casts

1. Evidence of past life, such as bones, teeth, and tracks, are ⬚.

2. Whole woolly mammoths have been preserved because they were ⬚.

3. Oil oozing above the ground made pools of ⬚, which preserved parts of animals.

4. Hardened sap from a tree can trap ⬚.

5. Wood becomes stone when it is ⬚.

6. Most fossils come from organisms that lived in the ⬚.

7. Many of the fossils people find are ⬚ and ⬚ of organisms.

8. Most fossils are ⬚ and are found in ⬚ rock.

Challenge!

1. If you found a bone in the soil, could you be sure it is a fossil? Why?

2. Why do you think fossils are not found in igneous rock?

3. Suppose a shellfish, such as a clam, dies and sinks to the bottom of the ocean. What might happen to the clam to stop it from becoming a fossil?

Science Words

cast

evidence

fossil

mold

petrify

preserve

Chapter 10
Fossils Tell a Story

The Tyrannosaurus shown here roamed the earth long, long ago. How do we know what this animal looked like? People were not around to draw pictures of dinosaurs. But fossils help tell us the story of these creatures.

The lessons in this chapter show ways you can learn about an organism by looking only at parts of the organism.

1 Completing a Puzzle

2 What Do Fossils Tell Us About Dinosaurs?

3 What Can People Learn from Fossil Evidence?

1 Completing a Puzzle

Most fossils that people find are only parts of an organism. If scientists find enough parts, they can put them together like pieces of a puzzle.

But how can scientists tell what a whole organism looked like from only a few parts? You can do an activity to help answer this question.

The picture shows several pieces of a puzzle. The pieces shown are in their right places. On a sheet of paper, draw how you think the whole organism looks.

Think About It

1. What animal does the picture show?
2. **Challenge** How did you know what the whole animal would look like?

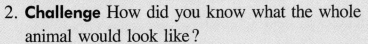

2 What Do Fossils Tell Us About Dinosaurs?

infer (in fėr′), to use what you already know to make a careful guess.

Find Out

Some scientists think *Brontosaurus* lived in the water, because water would help support its weight. But tracks and other clues suggest that it spent time out of the water. Look in the latest books on dinosaurs for new information.

Suppose you are putting together a jigsaw puzzle of a car. When you have fit the pieces together, you find that one is missing. Can you still tell what the car looks like?

You have seen cars before. You can use what you know to try to decide—or **infer**—how the car in the puzzle might look. Scientists use clues and experience to infer about the past.

The picture shows a fossil of the earliest known bird. People know a lot about birds today. Scientists infer that the ancient bird looked like the one in the drawing.

Scientists also use fossils to infer what dinosaurs were like. You may have seen dinosaur fossils in a museum. Fossils tell us that some dinosaurs were as small as chickens. Others were as large as houses. The next three pages describe a few kinds of dinosaurs and some things scientists have inferred about them.

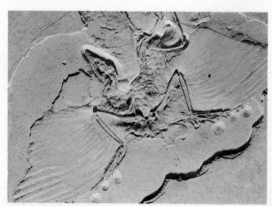
Fossil of earliest known bird

Drawing of earliest known bird

Brontosaurus (bron′tə sôr′əs) was one of the largest creatures that ever lived. These giants lived in swamps in the western United States. They ate only plants. As you can see, *Brontosaurus* had a small mouth compared to its large body. This dinosaur might have spent most of its time eating to stay alive.

Brontosaurus

Find Out

Use a dictionary to find out what the word *dinosaur* means.

How Were Dinosaurs Different from Each Other?

One of the small dinosaurs was *Protoceratops* (prō′tō ser′ə tops). It was only about two meters long. As the drawing shows, *Protoceratops* had a fan-shaped bone behind its head. This bone might have protected its neck from attack by other dinosaurs.

Dinosaurs laid eggs. The fossils in the picture are a nest of eggs laid by *Protoceratops*. Scientists have even found fossils that show baby *Protoceratops* hatching from the eggs.

A dinosaur that looked very fierce was *Tyrannosaurus* (ti ran′ə sôr′əs). These dinosaurs ate meat. They had large mouths and long, sharp teeth. But sometimes *Tyrannosaurus* had to fight long and hard for a meal.

Protoceratops eggs

Protoceratops

Other dinosaurs had ways to protect themselves from the meat eaters. As the picture shows, some dinosaurs had spikes and hard plates covering their bodies. If an enemy came too close, these dinosaurs gave it a whack with their large, bony tails.

Think About It

1. How do scientists infer what ancient plants and animals looked like?
2. **Challenge** Why do you think the teeth of *Tyrannosaurus* had to be sharper than the teeth of *Brontosaurus*?

Have You Heard?

The amount of meat *Tyrannosaurus* ate in one full bite would equal the amount of meat a human family of four might eat in a month.

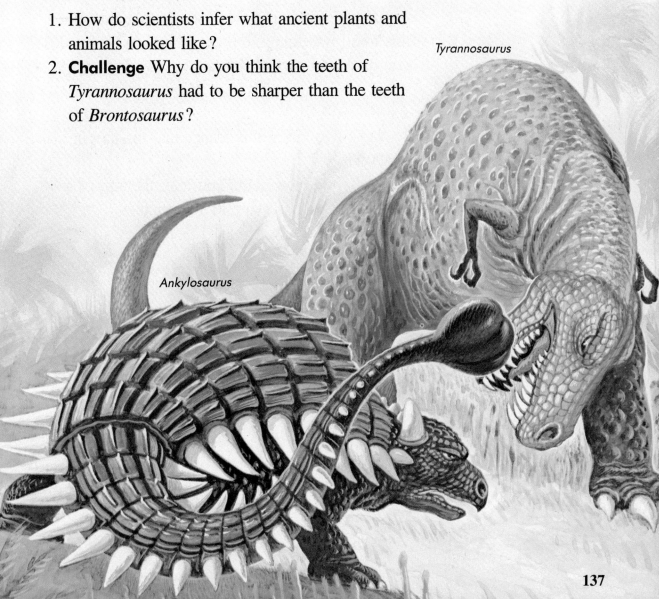

Tyrannosaurus

Ankylosaurus

137

3 What Can People Learn from Fossil Evidence?

A detective may study footprints when looking for a criminal. Scientists study footprints to learn more about the past.

The dinosaur footprints in the picture were made in mud. The mud later hardened into rock. The footprints tell what kind of dinosaur made them. What other clues are in the footprints?

Fossils can be clues to where ancient organisms' lived. The fossil shown is a fish. But this fossil was found in rocks in Kansas. What do you think that part of Kansas was like long ago?

Think About It

1. Name two kinds of evidence that fossils can show.
2. **Challenge** How could you infer the size of a dinosaur by observing its footprints?

Dinosaur footprints

Fossil fish in rock

Activity

Inferring What Made the Imprint

Purpose
To infer what object made an imprint.

You Will Need
- clay
- 7 or 8 small objects (pencil, paper clip, marble, and other objects)

Directions
1. Flatten a piece of clay, as shown.
2. As the other members of the group look away, use the objects to make several imprints in the clay. To make an imprint, push the object into the clay, as shown. Remove the object carefully.
3. Use as many objects and make as many imprints as you like. Some objects can make more than one kind of imprint. When you have made your imprints, lay the objects together on the desk.
4. Ask the other members of your group to infer which object made which imprint.
5. Take turns making the imprints, and repeat the activity.

Think About It

1. What objects were easiest to identify from their imprints?
2. Which objects were the hardest to identify from their imprints?
3. **Challenge** In this activity, what can you infer about imprints that are deeper than others?

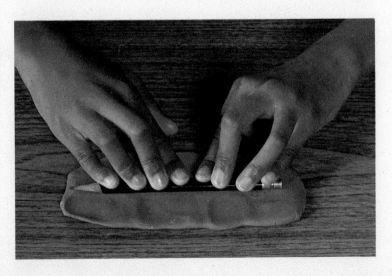

Do You Know?

Fossil Bones Are a Puzzle

Imagine finding a fossil bone that is taller than you are! Perhaps the bone belonged to a dinosaur. But people have never seen dinosaurs. How can we know how dinosaurs might have looked? Scientists piece together fossil bones to learn about dinosaurs.

Scientists look for fossils in the ground. When fossil bones are found, each bone is numbered. A drawing is made of the positions of the bones in the ground. The drawing might help scientists piece together the dinosaur skeleton.

Scientists then take the fossil bones out of the ground. First, they carefully dig around one of the bones. Second, they fix any cracks they find in the fossil's surface. Third, the bone is covered with sheets of wet paper and plaster. The plaster protects the bone. Finally, the bone is put into a shipping box. Scientists might even use a crane to lift the bone off the ground! The other fossil bones are dug up, covered with paper and plaster, and prepared for shipping to the laboratory.

When the fossil bones reach the laboratory, scientists clean the bones. Then, they study the bones' shapes to see how the bones might have fit together. Markings on the bones show where muscles might have been. The scientists use many clues to piece the skeleton together.

Scientists are always uncovering new clues about dinosaurs. The scientists in the picture have learned that this dinosaur skeleton probably wore the wrong head for many years. Years after the first bones of this kind of dinosaur were found, scientists found longer skull bones near a fossil of this dinosaur. Scientists think that the skull bones that were found later fit the dinosaur better than the first skull bones they found. Fossils can often tell us new things about the past.

Scientists changing dinosaur head

Tie It Together

Sum It Up

Look at the examples of two kinds of evidence. Imagine you were on a field trip and found this evidence. Write a report about what you saw. What can you infer from the evidence?

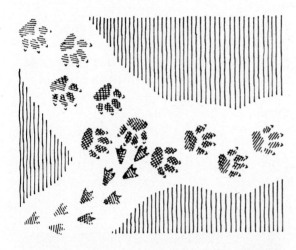

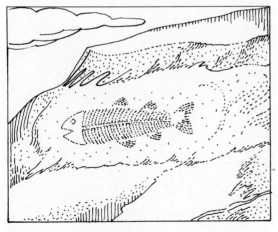

Challenge!

1. How is inferring different from guessing?

2. What evidence is there that *Brontosaurus* might have spent most of its time eating?

3. Look at the picture of *Tyrannosaurus* on page 137. What do you think it used its large tail for?

4. What kind of imprint would an ancient worm have made?

Science Word

infer

Laboratory

Inferring from Observations

Purpose
To infer the shape of an object from its remains.

You Will Need
• glue that will not dissolve in water
• 16 sugar cubes
• jar of water
• spoon

Stating the Problem
When an object wears away or decays, can its remains tell you something about the object? How can you use the remains to infer what the object looked like?

Investigating the Problem
1. Use waterproof glue to glue 8 sugar cubes together to make 1 large cube as shown in picture *a*. Let the glue dry.
2. Place your large cube in a jar of water. Using a spoon, stir gently until some of the sugar disappears, as shown in picture *b*.
3. Use a spoon to remove the remaining sugar from the water. Let the sugar dry. Observe what the remaining sugar looks like.

a

b

4. Take 8 more sugar cubes, and glue them into any design you like. Let the glue dry. Picture c shows examples of different designs you can make. On a sheet of paper, draw the sugar-cube design that you made.
5. Place the cubes in a jar of water. Gently stir until some of the sugar disappears.
6. Remove the remaining sugar, and let it dry. Observe what the remaining sugar design looks like. Compare it with the design that you drew.
7. Look at the remains of someone else's design. Infer what the design used to look like. Make a drawing that shows how the design used to look.

Making Conclusions

1. How could you use the remains of the sugar designs to infer what the designs used to look like?
2. Look at the design that has worn away on the statue in the picture. Can you infer from the remaining design what the design used to look like?
3. Compare the remains of the sugar cubes to animal remains, such as shells or bones. How can you use the remains of an organism to infer what that organism looked like in the past?

c

Careers

Fossil Preparator

Do you like to put together puzzles, or build models? Then you might like to have a job like Bill's. He is a preparator of fossils at a museum. Bill takes fossils out of rocks and cleans the fossils. He also fits bones together to form skeletons of animals.

"My interest in fossils began when I was seven years old," says Bill. "I had a set of plastic dinosaurs that I liked to play with."

When Bill went to college, he studied fossils. He also learned about the different parts of animals' bodies and how they work. "After all," says Bill, "you cannot put together animal bones if you do not know about all the parts of an animal."

Right now, Bill is working on some animals that scientists think died 55 million years ago! "The fossils show that these animals all died together. The fossils also show that the animals were about the size of cows and had hoofs. But we cannot say for sure why this group all died together. Maybe they were caught in a flood. Maybe they were swept away when they tried to cross a stream."

The block of stone that Bill is working on has about fifty bones in it. The bones are from about ten individual animals. "Out of all these bones, I may not find enough for one complete animal."

Bill uses a variety of tools, including chisels and brushes, to separate the rock from the fossil. He has to be careful because one wrong hit could break a valuable fossil instead of the rock.

"Studying fossils is very exciting. When I uncover a fossil from a rock, I am looking at something that no human has ever seen before!"

Anthropologist

Rock shop owner

Most fossils are the remains of plants and animals that lived millions of years ago. But some fossils are the bones of people that lived less than one million years ago.

Anthropologists (an/thrə pol/ə jists) look for fossils that show the remains of human life. They sometimes find bones, teeth, or entire skulls. These scientists try to infer how ancient people lived.

An anthropologist often uses the help of a **research assistant**. This person helps anthropologists and other scientists in many ways. The assistant may help discover and dig up fossils. He or she may then clean the fossils. Assistants also do research in a library.

Anthropologists and research assistants study in college. They learn about ancient people, fossils, and other areas of science.

If you want to look at fossils you could visit a museum. You could also go to a rock shop.

Here, you can buy fossils and unusual minerals. The **rock shop owner** may go on two or three digs each year to collect fossils and minerals for the shop. Sometimes, they sell or give a special fossil to a museum or college. Most people who work in rock shops enjoyed learning about fossils and minerals in school.

145

On Your Own

Picture Clue

To learn what happened to the animal in the picture on page 120, read the first paragraph on page 125 and look at the picture on that page.

Books About Science

Digging Up Dinosaurs by Aliki Brandenberg. Crowell Junior Books, 1981. Learn how scientists uncover, preserve, and study fossilized bones.

From Dinosaurs to Fossils by Annegert Fuchshuber. Carolrhoda Books Inc., 1981. This book shows you dinosaurs that ranged in sizes from very small to huge. This book tells what we know about these animals from their fossils.

If You Are a Hunter of Fossils by Bird Baylor. Charles Scribner's Sons, 1980. This is a story about hunting fossils that will take you on an imaginary trip back to the past.

Projects

1. Show some puzzles with missing pieces to a friend or to someone in your family. See if they can infer the rest of the picture. You could make a puzzle out of an old magazine picture by gluing the picture to stiff paper and cutting it into pieces. See who can infer the whole shape of an object by seeing the fewest pieces.

2. Prepare a "dig" for a friend. Ask permission to dig a small hole in your yard. Collect several small items to bury. They could be made of materials such as cotton or wool, paper, metal, plastic, plant matter, and bone. Bury one or two items under dirt, then bury one or two more. After all the items are buried, mark the spot with a rock or stick. After about two weeks, let a friend carefully uncover the items. Ask your friend what he or she can infer about each item.

3. Visit a library, and ask for the latest book, magazine article, or newspaper article about new fossil finds. Learn where the fossils were found and what organism they were part of. Find out if any fossils have been found near where you live.

Unit Test

Matching

Number your paper from 1–5. Read the description in Column I. Next to each number, write the word from Column II that best matches the description in Column I.

Column I

1. a clue that gives information about something
2. to turn to stone when minerals take the place of once-living matter
3. a preserved sign of life from the past
4. a hollow space where all or part of an organism was buried
5. to almost stop the decay of something that was once living

Column II

a. cast

b. mold

c. fossil

d. evidence

e. petrify

f. preserve

Multiple Choice

Number your paper from 6–9. Next to each number, write the letter of the word or words that best complete the statement.

6. A fossil is
   a. a decayed organism.
   b. any object found in rocks.
   c. evidence of past life.
   d. a very old object.

7. You can infer about something that happened in the past when
   a. you have no information.
   b. you have some evidence.
   c. a friend tells you his or her guess.
   d. there are no clues.

8. Organisms have been preserved in
   a. tar.
   b. hardened tree sap.
   c. ice.
   d. Answers a, b, and c are correct.

9. Fossil evidence of dinosaurs shows that
   a. dinosaurs were all huge.
   b. dinosaurs all ate meat.
   c. dinosaurs had many different shapes and sizes.
   d. dinosaurs all lived in water.

UNIT SIX
WATER

The city is a grand one
    indeed.
It stands high in the air.
Proud, yes.
Surrounded by a black
    blue sea.

Jeff Kuhnhenn *age 10*

Chapter 11
Water and the Weather

Clouds can float high above the earth or hang close to the ground. Sometimes clouds fill the sky and turn it a dull gray. There is water in the clouds in the picture. But even when the sky is clear and blue, there is water in the air.

The lessons in this chapter help you learn some reasons for changes in the weather.

1 Observing Changes in Water

2 Is Water in the Air?

3 Where Does Water Go?

1 Observing Changes in Water

The rainstorm is over, and the people in the picture want to play basketball. They decide to wait for the court to dry. As the wet spots disappear, the game begins. What happened to the water?

Wet a paper towel, and squeeze out the extra water. Then, use the paper towel to make a wet mark on the chalkboard. Observe the mark as it dries. Tear the towel into halves. Roll one half into a tight ball. Spread the other half out flat. As soon as the flattened half is dry, unfold the other half to see if it is dry.

Think About It

1. Where did the water go as the chalkboard dried?
2. **Challenge** Where did the water from the wet towels go? What do you think caused one half to dry faster?

2 Is Water in the Air?

evaporate (i vap′ə rāt′), change from a liquid into a gas.

water vapor (vā′pər), water in the air that is in the form of a gas.

condense (kən dens′), change from a gas into a liquid.

After you wash your hands, you dry them on a towel. The water moves from your hands to the towel. Does the water stay on the towel?

The water on the towel **evaporates**—or changes from a liquid to a gas. This gas—**water vapor**—becomes part of the air.

After you go swimming, the sun can dry your body. The sun's heat makes the water evaporate quickly from your body. Wind dries you too. The water becomes water vapor and mixes with air.

When water vapor cools, it may change back to a liquid—or **condense.** Water vapor is in the girl's warm breath. She breathes on the cool window, and the water vapor condenses. You can see the tiny water drops on the window.

Think About It

1. What happens to a puddle as it dries?
2. **Challenge** How could you make some water condense on a cold winter day?

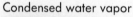
Condensed water vapor

Discover!

Camels Can Live Where There Is Little Water

Camel

Camel's nose passages

You could live only a few days if you did not have water to drink. Camels, which live in deserts, can live for weeks without drinking water. How can the camel live so long without water?

The answer, in part, can be found inside the camel's nose. To understand how the camel's nose helps the camel live in the desert, you need to understand what happens when you breathe out through your nose. For one thing you give off water as vapor. You can see the water when you breathe on a mirror. But not all the water in your breath goes into the air. Some of the water stays in damp passages inside your nose.

The camel, too, gives off water vapor when it breathes out through its nose. The passages inside a human's nose are short and fairly straight. But a camel's nose has long, twisting passages as shown in the drawing. Much of the water in a camel's breath is captured in these curled passages. The water stays inside a camel's nose, instead of escaping into the air.

With the help of its curled nose-passages, the camel saves water that it would lose from its breath. The camel's nose helps the camel live in the hot, dry desert.

3 Where Does Water Go?

Have You Heard?

You may have walked through a cloud. Fog is a cloud near the ground.

You know what a river looks like as it flows over the land. You can describe the clouds in the picture as a river of water in the sky.

Water evaporates from oceans, rivers, plants, your body, and other matter. **Evaporation** puts water vapor into the air. When the air cools, the vapor condenses into tiny drops of water. Clouds are drops of water that are condensed on specks of dust.

Sometimes these tiny drops of water join to form larger drops. When the drops get heavy enough, they may fall as rain.

Imagine following a drop of water as it falls during a rainstorm. The raindrop might first fall on a hillside. Then, it could roll into a stream. The stream could carry the drop along to a lake. The next day, the drop might evaporate into the air and become water vapor. Later that day, some vapor might condense back into a tiny drop, join a cloud, and fall again as rain.

The drop of water goes through the **water cycle** as it moves from one place to another. The drawing of the water cycle shows how the water on earth is used over and over.

Find Out

Use an atlas or almanac to find out which state in the United States receives the most rain. Find out how much rain your state receives.

water cycle (sī′kəl), path that water takes as it moves from one place to another.

Think About It

1. What is the water cycle?
2. **Challenge** Explain how the water you drink today might have been part of a cloud two weeks ago.

Water Cycle

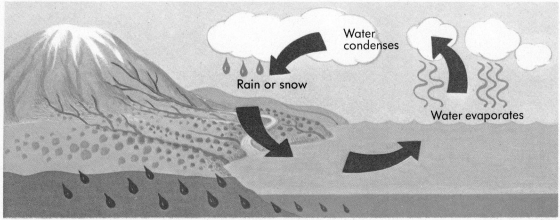

Water condenses

Rain or snow

Water evaporates

Activity

Observing Part of the Water Cycle

Purpose
To observe how water moves in the water cycle.

You Will Need
• large jar
• hot or warm water
• aluminum foil
• ice cubes

Directions
1. Half fill the jar with hot or warm water.
2. Place the foil over the opening of the jar. Press the aluminum foil lightly to make a bowl shape, as shown.
3. Place 2 or 3 ice cubes on the foil. Wait 10 minutes.
4. Remove the aluminum foil. Observe the bottom of the foil.

Think About It
1. What first happened to some of the hot water in the jar?
2. What did putting ice on the foil do to the warm air in the jar?
3. What was on the bottom of the foil when you removed it from the jar?
4. **Challenge** What part or parts of the water cycle were shown in this activity?

Tie It Together

Sum It Up

The drawing below shows the water cycle. Tell what is happening to the water at each number along the cycle.

Challenge!

1. How would you explain to someone that, every time you breathe, you take in water?

2. Why can we describe blowing clouds as a river of water in the sky?

3. Pretend that you are a water drop. Write a paragraph describing what you see as you fall as rain, evaporate, and travel around the world.

Science Words

condense

evaporate

evaporation

water cycle

water vapor

Chapter 12
Water, Water, Everywhere

Angel Falls, shown here, is the tallest waterfall in the world. This waterfall is part of a river in South America. At Angel Falls the river tumbles over the edge of a cliff and dives nearly 1,000 meters.

The lessons in this chapter tell you about different types of water and some ways people protect water supplies.

1 Describing Pathways of Water

If you took a trip in an airplane around the world, much of your time might be spent over water. Three-fourths of the earth's surface is covered by water.

Oceans are the largest bodies of water. Lakes and ponds are also bodies of water. Pathways of water include water that flows, such as a river or creek. Point out a body of water and a pathway of water in the picture.

Think of a body of water or a pathway of water near your school. Try to find a drawing of this water on a map.

Think About It

1. Is the body or pathway of water you chose on the map? What is the name of the water?
2. **Challenge** Name three bodies of water and three pathways of water on the earth.

2 Is All Water the Same?

salt water, water that contains a lot of salt.

You may have heard stories about people who were shipwrecked. People have spent days drifting on the ocean in a lifeboat. They were probably very thirsty. But they could not drink the ocean water.

Water contains different kinds and amounts of minerals. Ocean water contains a lot of the mineral salt. Ocean water is **salt water.** The salt water of the Caribbean Sea in the picture may be refreshing for swimming. But salt water is harmful to drink.

Salt water

Much of the oceans' salt comes from rock beneath the ocean floor. Salt and other minerals in the rock slowly mix with the water. As surface water evaporates, the salt stays behind, making the ocean salty.

Some of the salt for our dinner tables comes from the ocean. The picture shows some of the salt that was left behind after shallow ocean water evaporated.

Find Out

Look up *Mono Lake* in an encyclopedia. Find out what is happening to the water there.

Salt after evaporation

Where Do We Get Fresh Water?

Fresh water is water that has very little salt. Nearly all the water we use is fresh water. We get this water from rivers, ponds, lakes, and from under the ground.

Most of our fresh water comes from rain or melting snow. In spring, melting snow adds clear, fresh water to streams, as shown.

Many people get their fresh water from lakes. Sometimes people change parts of a river into a lake by building a dam. The dam in the picture blocks the flowing water. Water collects behind the dam and is stored for many uses.

Have you Heard?

Most of the earth's fresh water is frozen in glaciers.

Stream with melting snow

Dam at San Carlos Lake

Some fresh water from rain, rivers, and lakes soaks into the ground. The water fills the spaces between and within pieces of rock under the ground. To get to this **groundwater,** people can dig a well such as the one in the drawing. The children are using a pump to bring well water to the surface.

groundwater, water that fills the spaces between and within pieces of underground rock.

Think About It

1. How does salt get into ocean water?
2. Name four places we can find fresh water.
3. **Challenge** What might happen if a lot of water were pumped out of the ground during a year when there was little rainfall to soak back into the ground?

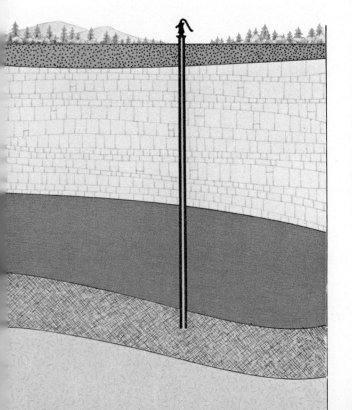

Well

Children getting water from a well

Activity

Comparing Salt Water and Fresh Water

Purpose
To compare how objects float in salt water and in fresh water.

You Will Need
- plastic cup
- salt
- water
- spoon
- 2 pie tins or shallow pans
- 2 corks or other light objects of the same size that will float
- several pennies or washers (optional)

Directions
1. Fill the cup about half full with water. Mix the water with 2 spoonfuls of salt.
2. Pour the salt water into a pie tin. Place the same amount of plain tap water in the other pie tin.
3. Gently place 1 cork in each pie tin. Keep the corks from the edges of the pie tins. Observe which cork floats higher in the water.
4. Switch the corks. Now which one floats higher?
5. If the corks or other objects are flat, begin placing washers or pennies on top, as shown. Find out which type of water holds up the heaviest cork.

Think About It
1. Did one of the corks float higher than the other? In which type of water was that cork?
2. **Challenge** Which do you think is heavier, salt water or fresh water?

164

Do You Know?

How Does Water Get to the Faucets in Your Home?

Fresh water from faucet

Years ago, many people did not have indoor water faucets. They might have carried their water from a well or pump outdoors. But you probably do not leave your home to get your water. For you, water flows out of an open faucet. Where does that water come from? You can use the picture to follow the path that the water might take to your home.

Your water might come from under the ground or from a lake or river. But the water might be dirty and contain harmful organisms. So the water must be cleaned.

Large pipes carry water to a water treatment plant. There, the water is made pure for drinking. It is sent through long tubes of sand and charcoal that remove dirt. Chemicals are added to kill the harmful organisms.

When the water is safe to drink, it travels to a storage area. Large pipes carry the water from the storage area to the town. Smaller pipes branch off from the large pipe and carry the water to buildings. Pipes inside the buildings bring water to the faucets. When you open the faucet, the water flows, as shown in the picture.

Your water might travel a long way before it flows through your faucet, clean and sparkling.

Water's path to town

165

3 Why Should We Protect Our Water Supply?

Think of all the times you use water during the day. Now, imagine what the day would be like if your water supply were suddenly gone.

People need water for drinking, cooking, washing, and growing crops. There are many ways people use and enjoy clean water. People are learning to use water wisely because water is so important. Using water wisely means keeping it clean and using only as much as we need.

Canoeing

Fishing

Sailing

Scuba diving

Look at the water-treatment plant in the picture. At this plant, garbage, disease organisms, and other harmful materials are removed from water before people use the water. Many cities and factories also clean water after it is used.

Think About It

1. Give two reasons for using water wisely.
2. **Challenge** How could garbage that has been dumped on land end up in our water?

Water treatment plant

4 How Is Water Different?

hard water, water that contains a lot of minerals.

soft water, water that contains few or no minerals.

Have You Heard?

Ocean salmon find the freshwater river in which they hatched by smelling and tasting the river water as it flows into the ocean.

Fresh water around the world contains different amounts and kinds of minerals. Not all fresh water is the same.

Hard water has a lot of minerals. Minerals give water its taste and sometimes a little color. Minerals in hard water might stain tubs and sinks.

Soft water has fewer minerals than hard water. Soft water, such as rain, makes your skin feel smooth and slippery. People in some places collect rain in water buckets, as shown. Many people like to use soft water because it makes suds easily when mixed with soap. Soft water has no color and does not leave stains.

Think About It

1. Name and define two kinds of fresh water.
2. **Challenge** How could you test water from two different places to find out which one is the softest?

Water bucket with rain water

Tie It Together

Sum It Up

Two kinds of water are described below. Number your paper from 1–5. Write fresh water or salt water after each number.

1. Has very little salt

2. Has too much salt to drink

3. Comes from rivers and lakes

4. Rain

5. Leaves a certain mineral behind when it evaporates

Each phrase below describes hard water or soft water. Number your paper from 6–10. Name the kind of fresh water each phrase describes.

6. Has a certain taste

7. Stains tubs and sinks

8. Makes suds easily when mixed with soap

9. Has a lot of minerals in it

10. Does not stain clothes

Challenge!

1. New York City is near the Atlantic Ocean. Do you think New York City uses the Atlantic Ocean for its water supply? Give your reasons.

2. Groundwater is usually hard water. From where do you think the minerals in groundwater come?

3. Describe how your day might be different from normal if you could not use water the whole day.

4. Why might people want water softeners in their homes?

Science Words

fresh water

groundwater

hard water

salt water

soft water

Laboratory

Condensation and Evaporation

Purpose
To measure changes in the weight of a sealed jar of water to show what happens when condensation and evaporation take place.

You Will Need
- paper punch
- aluminum foil
- 2 sealed baby-food jars, filled with equal amounts of water that has been dyed with red food coloring
- an equal-arm balance
- freezer

Stating the Problem
When a glass of ice water sits outside on a hot day, the glass quickly becomes coated with drops of water. From where does the water come? Some of the water on the outside of the glass may disappear. Where does the water go?

Investigating the Problem
1. Use a paper punch to punch 30 holes into a sheet of aluminum foil. Save the circles of aluminum foil that you punched out.
2. Place a sealed jar of colored water on each pan of a balance.
3. The jars should be balanced, as shown in picture *a*. If not, open the jars, and add water to the jars to balance them. Then, seal the jars.

a

4. Remove both jars from the balance. Place one of the jars in a freezer for about 30 minutes.
5. Remove the jar from the freezer. After a few minutes, observe the outside of the jar. Record your observations.
6. Pick up the jars by their lids, and place both jars on the balance. Observe the movement of the balance.
7. As shown in picture *b,* add some aluminum circles to either side of the balance to keep the jars balanced. Record how many circles you added.
8. Let the jars stay on the balance until the water on the outside of the cooled jar disappears.
9. When the water disappears, remove the aluminum circles you added to the balance. The jars should be balanced once again.

Making Conclusions
1. How did the weight of the jar of water change after you cooled the jar? How do you know?
2. From where did the water on the outside of the cooled jar come?
3. Where did the water on the jar go?
4. How do you know that the amount of water on the outside of the cooled jar was equal to the amount of water that disappeared?

b

Careers

Water-Softener Installer

When you take a drink of water, does it have an unpleasant taste? Does water leave red stains from the faucet down the side of the sink? "Maybe you need a water softener," says Bruce.

Bruce installs and repairs water softeners. Certain minerals in water, such as iron and calcium, give water a funny taste and smell. A water softener removes some of the minerals.

"The first thing I do is test the water to see how hard it is. Water with a lot of minerals is called hard water. After testing the water, I know what kind of equipment to install. The main piece of water-softening equipment is a tank. Water goes into the tank where chemicals are added. These

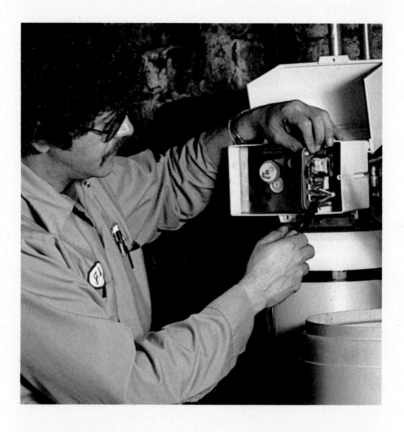

chemicals remove minerals from the water. The kind and amount of chemicals used depends on the water's hardness.

"When the water comes out of your faucet, it tastes better and does not stain the sink."

To install the softener, Bruce has to know a lot about plumbing. He

cuts and installs pipes, and he has to be sure they go to the right places. "I like working with my hands and putting things together. I also like knowing that I help people enjoy pure, healthy water."

You probably handle water every day. You might drink it, swim in it, or wash with it. For some people, water is a big part of their jobs.

Water treatment plant operators make sure the water we use is clean and safe. They control the machines that purify the water from lakes and streams. The operators learn how to read special meters and run the machines while training on the job.

Another person who works with water is an **oceanographer**. This person may do many exciting things while learning about the ocean. An oceanographer may scuba dive to learn about coral and tropical fish. This person might also ride in special submarines to explore the bottom of the sea. Most oceanographers spend some time at sea but these scientists also

Water treatment plant operator

Oceanographer

work on land.

If you want to be an oceanographer, you must go to college for four years.

Do you think you may enjoy spending some time on the ocean? If so, you might like to be a **U.S. Coast Guard member**. The Coast Guard works to make the seas safe.

They may warn ships of icebergs, stop criminals in boats, or rescue people at sea. The Coast Guard is part of the military. Members serve from one to four years. The first nine weeks are spent at a training camp.

On Your Own

Picture Clue

To find out about the structures on page 148, read page 161. For the name of the lake, look at the "Find Out" in the margin of page 161.

Books About Science

Fog in the Meadow by Joanne Ryder. Harper and Row, 1979. This is a story about animals in a meadow and how they were hidden from each other in the fog.

Pictures and Pollution by Barbara Slavin Kataoka. Children's Press, 1977. Works of art show what pollution does to the land and to people.

The Weather by Frank Dalton. Priory Press, 1977. This story tells how scientists gather weather information and how the weather forecasters use the information to make predictions.

Projects

1. Look at a map to find bodies of water and roads in your area. If possible, visit a library, and compare a very old map of your area with an up-to-date map. Look for any changes in the bodies of water and in the roads.

2. Use a microscope. Find three or four sources of water, such as the ocean, a lake, rain, a pond, a stream or river, a well, and water from a tap. Put drops of water from your sources on a glass slide. Let the water evaporate. Observe which drop left the most minerals on the slide and whether any of the drops left no minerals.

3. Compare how well soap makes suds in different kinds of water. Ask for water without minerals—distilled water. Compare a cupful of distilled water with a cupful of tap water and with a cupful of water to which one spoonful of salt was added. Put one squirt of liquid soap in each cup. Swish the water or shake it up to see which water makes the best suds.

Unit Test

Matching

Number your paper from 1–5. Read the description in Column I. Next to each number, write the word or words from Column II that best match the description in Column I.

Column I

1. water that contains a lot of minerals
2. to change from a liquid to a gas
3. water found in most rivers and lakes
4. changing of water from vapor to liquid and back to vapor, over and over
5. to change from a gas to a liquid

Column II

a. condense

b. evaporate

c. fresh water

d. groundwater

e. hard water

f. water cycle

Multiple Choice

Number your paper from 6–10. Next to each number, write the letter of the word or words that best complete the statement.

6. Water under the ground
   a. dissolves minerals in the ground.
   b. is always clean.
   c. comes from the ocean.
   d. never flows into lakes or streams.

7. Salt water, rain, and hard water
   a. all have the same properties.
   b. all taste the same.
   c. all are condensed water.
   d. all have the same minerals.

8. In the water cycle
   a. there are different kinds of water.
   b. water changes form.
   c. water travels from place to place.
   d. Answers a, b, and c are correct.

9. You can always find salt water in
   a. ponds.   c. lakes.
   b. rivers.   d. oceans.

10. Clean water
   a. can always be found in lakes.
   b. is a valuable resource.
   c. is only found under the ground.
   d. Answers a, b, and c are correct.

UNIT SEVEN
PROTECTION
AND DEFENSE IN
LIVING THINGS

The little moth
    sits there so still.
And looks just like
    a leaf.
The thing
    that gives him away
Are his antennas.

Bern Hart *age 10*

Chapter 13
Coverings
That Protect

This young harp seal lives in a dangerous, icy world. Killer whales and polar bears hunt it for food. But the seal's white fur coat helps keep it hidden. The seal is hard to see on the ice and snow. The fur coat also helps keep the seal warm.

The lessons in this chapter will show you some of the ways body coverings are important in the lives of animals.

1 Observing Animal Coverings

2 How Do Coverings Protect Animals?

3 How Do Colors and Patterns Help Animals?

1 Observing Animal Coverings

All animals have skin that covers their bodies. Skin helps protect their bodies.

Some animals' skins have extra protection, such as shells and feathers. Notice the coverings on the animals in the pictures. List at least three different kinds of animal coverings you have seen. Next, choose an animal not shown in the pictures. Draw your animal, and show its covering.

Think About It

1. List five outer coverings animals can have.
2. **Challenge** Explain how your animal's body covering might help protect it.

Armadillo

Peacock

2 How Do Coverings Protect Animals?

predator (pred′ə tər), an animal that hunts, kills, and eats other animals.

If you play a sport, you might wear knee guards, elbow guards, or a helmet. These things cover and protect parts of your body.

Animals have outer coverings protecting their bodies. The turtle in the picture has a shell that helps keep its soft parts from getting hurt. A shell also protects a turtle from **predators**—animals that want to eat other animals.

Many animals have hard outer coverings on their bodies. Notice the coverings on the shrimp, lobsters, and crabs in the picture. Predators cannot easily bite through these coverings. The sharp points on the sea urchin's body keep predators from coming too close.

Green turtle

Shrimp

Spiny lobster

Coral crab

Long-spined sea urchin

Scales are thin, round pieces of hard matter. They protect the bodies of many animals. Notice the scales covering the snake's body. When a snake crawls, its scales keep it from getting scratched. The scales also make a snake's body waterproof and help keep it from drying out.

The hippopotamus and rhinoceros in the pictures live and grow in different places—or **habitats.** A hippopotamus lives in hot, wet places. A rhinoceros lives in grasslands that are hot and dry. But these animals have the same kind of protective covering. The thick, tough skin covering their bodies helps protect them from injuries.

Adder snake

Have You Heard?
Snakes often grow new skins. When a rattlesnake crawls out of its old skin, a ring of that skin stays on its tail. Rings of old skins harden and become rattles.

habitat (hab′ə tat), the place where a plant or animal lives.

Hippopotamuses

Black rhinoceros

How Do Fur and Feathers Help Protect Animals?

Have You Heard?
Down jackets, quilts, vests, and pillows are stuffed with the light, fluffy inner feathers of birds.

Fur and feathers help keep animals warm. Notice the fur on the musk ox in the picture. A shaggy outer layer of hair covers a thick inner layer of fur. The fur coat traps the body heat close to the skin of the animal. Trapped body heat keeps the musk ox warm in its freezing habitat.

The snowy owl in the picture has a thick covering of soft, fluffy feathers. The owl can fluff its feathers to make more space between them for trapping air. The trapped air keeps the animal's body heat from escaping.

Think About It

1. Explain how different kinds of body coverings protect animals.
2. **Challenge** Some animals live where it is cold in winter and hot in summer. What happens to their fur in the summer?

Musk ox

Snowy Owl

Do You Know?

How Does a Bird Care for Its Feathers?

Bird preening its feathers

Ancient Aztec Indians in Mexico made colorful jewelry out of bird feathers. These Indians thought bird feathers were more valuable than gold. As valuable as feathers were to some people, feathers are much more valuable to birds.

Feathers help a bird fly and keep warm. So a bird must keep its feathers in good shape.

Birds spend a lot of time cleaning and straightening—or preening—their feathers. The bird in the picture is preening its feathers. The bird uses its beak to separate and smooth each feather. Under the bird's skin are pockets of oil. The bird uses its beak to spread oil over each feather. The oil helps keep the feathers clean.

Oil is especially important to water birds, such as ducks and geese. Oil makes feathers waterproof. Feathers that are not waterproof soak up water. Birds with soaked feathers become heavy and sink in water. Water birds spend many hours each day waterproofing their feathers with oil.

Even if a bird preens carefully, feathers do not stay healthy forever. So every bird grows a new set of feathers at least once a year. When a bird's feathers fall out, we say that the bird is molting. After a bird molts, new feathers grow in.

Most birds molt a few feathers at a time throughout the year. That is why you can often find feathers here and there on the ground.

3 How Do Colors and Patterns Help Animals?

camouflage
(kam/ə fläzh), a color or pattern that keeps an animal from being easily seen.

prey (prā), an animal hunted for food.

When you play some games, you hide. But animals are not playing games when they hide. Some animals hide from predators. Others hide to catch their food.

Look carefully at the frog in the picture. Notice how it blends with its habitat. Colors and patterns that help animals blend with their surroundings are **camouflage.** A frog's color is the frog's camouflage. It helps a frog hide from its predators.

Patterns also help animals hide. The tiger in the picture is hunting **prey**—an animal it uses for food. The picture shows how the tiger's stripes blend with the up-and-down lines of the grass. The tiger's striped coat is its camouflage in the tall grass. The prey will not see the tiger until the tiger is very close. If it saw the tiger, it would run away.

Frog in its habitat

Tiger in its habitat

Colors and patterns do not always hide animals. Some animals, such as the skunk in the picture, have colors and patterns that give warnings. Skunks spray predators with a bad-smelling liquid. Once an animal is hit by a skunk's spray, it stays away from all other skunks.

Many animals have colors and patterns that scare predators. The butterfly in the picture has a spot on each wing that looks like a larger animal's eye. If a predator comes near, the butterfly's spot often surprises and frightens the predator away.

Think About It

1. Explain how colors and patterns help animals.
2. **Challenge** How do nature photographers dress when they want to get close to animals?

Find Out

The bodies of many fish are dark colored on top and light colored on the bottom. How does this coloring protect them from predators?

Striped skunk

Caligo butterfly

185

Activity

Observing Animals Using Camouflage

Purpose
To show how animals use camouflage.

You Will Need
• white drawing paper
• crayons
• scissors

Directions
1. Draw and cut out an animal that uses camouflage.
2. Draw your animal's habitat and another habitat that is very different.
3. Place your animal in its habitat, as in the picture. Then, place your animal in the other habitat.

Think About It

1. With which habitat did your animal blend?
2. In which habitat did your animal stand out?
3. **Challenge** What would you wear to camouflage yourself in each habitat? Place a drawing of yourself in each habitat.

Tie It Together

Sum It Up

Look at the animal pictures. Number a paper from 1–4. Next to each number write a sentence explaining how the animal's covering helps protect it.

1. Sea urchin

2. Musk ox

3. Striped skunk

4. Tree frog

Challenge!

1. How does a porcupine's covering help protect it?

2. How do people dress to protect themselves from different types of weather?

3. List animals in your neighborhood that use camouflage.

Science Words

camouflage

habitat

predator

prey

Chapter 14
Animal Defenses

Most fish do not protect their young. They lay their eggs and leave. But this fish protects its young from danger. It holds them in its mouth until the danger is over.

The lessons in this chapter will tell about some actions animals use to protect themselves.

1 Observing How Animals Protect Their Young or Each Other

Some animals protect their young. Some even protect other adults of their own kind.

Look at these animal pictures. On a sheet of paper, write the numbers 1 to 3. Next to each number, write one or two sentences explaining what you think is happening in each picture. Then, look in magazines and books to find pictures of animals protecting their own kind.

Grey kangaroos

Think About It

1. Describe three ways animals take care of their young or each other.
2. **Challenge** Think of ways people protect each other.

Great blue herons

African elephants

2 Why Do Some Animals Run and Hide?

Not all animals have hard shells, sharp spines, or scary colors to keep predators away. Some animals move very quickly, and some hide.

The healthy antelope in the picture can run so fast that they escape most predators. An antelope can run as fast as a car traveling on a highway. Other animals, such as deer and rabbits, also run from predators.

A spider monkey does not run from its predators when it is in danger. It very quickly climbs high up into a tree. Notice how the spider monkey carries its baby on its back to protect the baby from predators.

Birds and many insects can fly away from most predators. A sparrow can fly away from a cat. Moths try to fly away from bats.

Pronghorn antelope

Spider monkey

Many animals hide from predators. Moles, badgers, and prairie dogs dig holes in the ground—or **burrows.** Notice the burrows in this picture of a prairie dog town. Even when the dogs are feeding or playing, they are always watching for predators. If a predator comes near, the first dog to see it gives a warning bark. Then, the prairie dogs race in all directions to hide in their burrows.

Insects and worms often hide in small openings in trees, rocks, or buildings. If you turn over a rock, you might find these small animals hiding under it.

burrow (bėr′ō), hole dug in the ground by an animal.

Think About It

1. Name some animals that move very quickly to get away from predators.
2. **Challenge** Suppose an animal cannot move away or hide from predators. What might an animal do to stop predators from eating it?

Find Out

How close can you get to a bird before it flies away? Try to measure the distance with a meter stick.

Prairie dog town

Activity

Observing Prey Protecting Themselves

Purpose
To observe how prey use their hearing to protect themselves from predators.

You Will Need
• large open space in which to play a game
• groups of five people
• blindfold

Directions
1. Five people should join hands and form a circle.
2. The people should drop hands, and take 10 steps backward.
3. One person should go to the center of the circle and pretend to be the prey. The prey should be blindfolded, as in the picture.
4. The people forming the circle should take turns pretending to be predators.
5. A predator should try to get close to the prey without being heard.
6. If the prey hears the predator, it points toward the predator and calls, "Stop." If the prey is pointing directly at the predator, the predator must leave the game.
7. But if the predator tags the prey, the predator calls, "Stop." Then the prey must leave the game, and the predator takes its place.
8. The game ends when only one person is left.

Think About It

1. How must the predators in the game move so that they might catch the prey?
2. **Challenge** How can the prey move their bodies to help them more easily hear the predators?

Do You Know?

Some Animals Are Actors

Kildeer bluffing

Which animal is stronger, a big snake or a small mouse? You probably answered that the snake is stronger. And you are probably right. A mouse must defend itself from snakes which eat mice.

A mouse usually tries to run away and hide when it sees a snake. But sometimes a mouse defends itself in a different way. It stands still and pretends it is going to attack the snake. The mouse's actions might scare or confuse the snake.

When an animal acts this way we say it is bluffing. A mouse might use bluffing when it is too far from its home to make a quick getaway.

Many animals, when bluffing, look larger and fiercer than normal. You probably have seen a cat raise its back, fluff its fur, and hiss when a dog comes near it. With its raised back and fur standing on end, the cat looks larger than normal. The dog might back off from the fierce, hissing cat.

But not all animals use bluffing to frighten their enemies. When a predator approaches, the killdeer bird protects the young in its nest by pretending that its wing is broken, as shown in the picture. By bluffing, the killdeer draws attention away from its nest of helpless young birds. If the predator follows the bird away from the nest, the young birds might be safe. The bluffing killdeer then flies to safety.

3 How Do Animals Use Teeth, Beaks, Claws, Hoofs, or Poisons?

poisonous (poi′zn əs), full of poison.

Have You Heard?

Anteaters tear insect nests apart with their long, sharp, curved claws. Then, they catch their prey by putting their long, sticky tongues into the nests.

Many animals use sharp teeth, beaks, claws, or hoofs to catch prey or to protect themselves. Notice the claws on the eagle in the picture. Eagles try to surprise prey on the ground. They come down suddenly on their prey and grip it tightly in their strong claws. If an eagle is attacked on the ground, it lies on its back and sticks out its claws.

Some animals use poison to catch prey. When a rattlesnake bites its prey, it sends poison into the prey's body. Many spiders have a harmful—or **poisonous**—bite.

Think About It

1. Name some body parts that animals use to catch prey or to protect themselves.
2. **Challenge** Compare a kitten's claws with the eagle's claws in the picture. Tell how they are alike or different.

Bald eagle

194

Tie It Together

Sum It Up

Draw a picture to go with each statement.

1. Some animals protect their young.

2. Some animals escape predators by moving very quickly.

3. Some animals hide from predators.

4. Some animals use claws to catch prey.

Challenge!

1. Name some animals that do not protect their young.

2. Find out where animals hide in your neighborhood.

3. How do soldier ants protect their nests?

Science Words

burrow

poisonous

Chapter 15
Plants

Have you ever seen giant carrots? The trees in this Boojum forest remind some people of carrots. The heavy trunks store water for these desert plants. Their leaves last a few weeks after a rain. Then the stems turn into thorns.

The lessons in this chapter will show how different coverings and unusual ways of growing help plants stay alive.

1 Inventing a Plant Covering

2 How Can Some Plants Harm People?

3 What Are Some Unusual Ways Plants Grow?

1 Inventing a Plant Covering

Many plants that grow in dry habitats store water in their stems. Some animals try to eat these plants to get the water that is stored in them. The pictures show plants that live in dry habitats. Explain how their coverings protect them from being eaten by animals.

Invent a new and unusual covering for a plant. Make a model of your plant, and explain how its covering protects it.

Think About It

1. In what ways is your model like a real plant you know about?
2. **Challenge** How might small animals use some plant coverings as hiding places?

Plants that live in dry habitats

2 How Can Some Plants Harm People?

The coverings on some plants help protect the plants from being eaten. But these plant coverings can harm you. The poison ivy and stinging nettle plants, shown in the picture, have parts covered with poison. If you touch one of these plants, your skin might burn, sting, or itch.

Some house and garden plants can make you ill if you eat them. The dumb cane, philodendron (fil/ə den/drən), and holly plants have poisonous parts. Never taste plant parts unless you know they are safe to eat.

Think About It

1. Explain how some plants can harm you.
2. **Challenge** Make a list of harmful plants.

Poison ivy

Stinging nettle

Dumb cane

Philodendron

Holly

Do You Know?

Many Wild Plants Are Good to Eat

Dandelion salad

Cattails

American Indians and early pioneers cooked delicious meals without ever stepping inside a grocery store. They collected and cooked wild plants. Even if you live in a city, wild plants might grow nearby. You can learn to make some of these plants into marvelous meals.

Cattails, which grow in swampy places, as shown in the picture, can be used in many ways. The roots of cattail plants can be eaten raw, baked, or roasted. Or you can dry the roots and grind them into flour. Bread and cake can be made from this flour.

The stalks of the cattail are also good to eat. You can peel off the outer layer and cook the white inside-part. The cooked stalks taste like asparagus.

The dandelion, which might grow in your yard, is another wild plant that can be used to make many fine meals. Dandelion leaves make delicious salads. The green buds of dandelion flowers can be cooked and eaten in soups or with eggs. Dandelion roots can be roasted, ground, and used in making a hot drink.

Many other wild plants are good to eat. But some wild plants can make you very sick if you eat them. Other plants might have been sprayed with poison. Before you pick a plant, find out from an adult if the plant is safe for you to eat. If it is safe, you might make a meal that could have been found on the plates of American Indians and pioneers.

3 What Are Some Unusual Ways Plants Grow?

Find Out

Use an encyclopedia to find out how the roots of mangrove trees grow and help form islands in the ocean.

All green plants need light, water, and other nutrients. The plants in some habitats grow in unusual ways so they can get these things.

The trees in a rain forest grow very tall and close together. Their leaves block the sun so that very little light reaches the ground below. But liana (lē ä′nə) vines growing in the forest still get light. The picture shows how they grow up the trunks of trees to the very top of the forest. Lianas, like many other plants, have tubes inside their stems. The tubes carry water from the soil to the leaves and flowers high above.

Many other plants get sun because they grow high up on the trunks and branches of trees. Notice how some of the leaves on the staghorn fern grow in the shape of a cup. During a rain, the fern stores water in its cups. It has no roots in the ground.

Liana vines

Staghorn fern

Plants need nutrients to help them grow. Most plants get the nutrients they need from the ground. But the soil in bogs has very little of these nutrients. So some bog plants trap insects and get the nutrients from the insects' bodies. Notice the hairs covering the leaves on the sundew plant. If an insect touches one of these sticky hairs, it becomes stuck. The hairs hold the insect until the plant is ready to use it.

Think About It

1. How do plants in a forest grow to get the most light possible?
2. How do some plants attract and eat insects to get nutrients?
3. **Challenge** Tell how the roots of dandelions and grass are different. Which plant gets water near the surface of the ground?

Have You Heard?

Spanish moss is a plant that grows on telephone lines and the branches of trees. It gets its water from the air and makes its own food.

Sundew plant

Activity

Observing the Growth of Plant Stems

Purpose
To observe that plant stems grow toward a light source.

You Will Need
- potting soil
- small paper cup (about 5 cm in diameter)
- large paper cup (about 8 cm in diameter)
- radish seed
- medicine dropper
- pencil
- container of water

Directions
1. Use a pencil to punch a hole through the side of the large cup. Make the hole near the top of the cup, as in the picture.
2. Put some potting soil in a small paper cup. Make the layer of soil about 2 cm high.
3. Place a radish seed on top of the soil.
4. Cover the radish seed with a layer of soil about 1 cm high.
5. Put about 10 drops of water in the small cup. Keep the soil in the cup moist.
6. When the radish stem reaches the rim of the cup, cover the plant and cup with the large cup. The picture shows you how.
7. Observe your plant for a few days.

Think About It
1. What do you observe about the radish stem?
2. **Challenge** Look for plants in your home or neighborhood whose stems are growing in unusual ways. Describe how the stems are growing.

Tie It Together

Sum It Up

Look at the pictures and read the sentences. Number your paper from 1–3. Write the letter of the picture next to the number of the sentence that explains it.

a Liana vine

b Stinging nettle

c Holly

1. A plant that is poisonous if eaten.

2. A plant that can harm you if you touch it.

3. A plant that grows in an unusual way to get light.

Challenge!

1. What defenses do the plants have where you live?

2. Why should you never burn poison ivy plants?

3. What kinds of plant parts do some plants have that help them live in the water?

Laboratory

Protective Coloring

Purpose
To show how the color of an animal affects its safety.

You Will Need
- meter stick
- 4 large nails
- string, 17 m long
- 50 plain wooden toothpicks
- 50 green-colored toothpicks
- clock with second hand

Stating the Problem
A hawk circles above a field, looking for food. One brown rabbit sits on a pile of dried leaves. Another brown rabbit sits in green grass. The hawk dives and catches the rabbit in the grass. Why was it easier for the hawk to catch the rabbit that was in the grass? Both rabbits were the same color. Neither rabbit moved. Why was the rabbit next to the leaves safe that time?

Investigating the Problem
1. Go outside to a grassy area.
2. Make a square in the grass as shown in picture a. Each side of your square should be 4-m long. Stick a nail into the ground at each corner of your square. Wrap string around the nails to make the edges of your square.
3. Do steps 3–6 with a partner. Have your partner look the other way. Then, take 50 green toothpicks and 50 plain toothpicks, and scatter them in the square. See picture b.
4. Give your partner 30 seconds to find as many toothpicks as he or she can. Tell your partner when to start looking.
5. After 30 seconds, say "Stop." Help count the number of plain toothpicks that your partner found.

a

b

Help count the number of green toothpicks that your partner found. Write down these numbers.

6. Make a new square, and ask your partner to scatter the toothpicks, as in step 3. Ask your partner to time you for 30 seconds. Pick up as many toothpicks as you can. Write down the number of each color of toothpick that you found.

7. Make a chart that shows the numbers of plain and green toothpicks which each student picked up. See picture c.

Making Conclusions

1. Compare the numbers of plain and of green toothpicks that each student found. If there are differences in the numbers, how do you explain the differences?

Name	Number of plain toothpicks	Number of green toothpicks

c

2. Suppose you were a bird. Suppose the toothpicks were insects. Which insects would be easier for you to find? Why?

3. Suppose you were an insect. How would your color protect you from birds that eat insects? If you lived in the grass, which color would keep you the safest? Why?

4. Find the 2 moths in the picture. Which moth would be safer from the birds that eat moths?

5. Find the polar bear in the picture. How would the polar bear's white color help the bear get its food?

Moths on tree

Polar bear

Careers

Wildlife Manager

"Once we had a sandhill crane who sounded more like a goose," says Chet. "The crane kept honking at everyone. We tried to get it a mate. But the crane honked at her too! Finally, this spring, the crane found its own mate and they left together. Maybe someday they will come back for a visit."

Taking care of cranes and other birds is just one of Chet's jobs as the wildlife manager of a nature center. He also talks to the people who visit the center. "Many of our visitors are from nearby cities and suburbs," says Chet. "They really enjoy strolling along our trails through the woods. I tell them what animals to look for along the trails."

Chet has seen many changes at the nature center over the past few years. "As more and more people build homes near the nature center, many animals move away. Also, hunters sometimes shoot hawks and falcons. These birds are getting harder and harder to find.

"But some changes are good. The cornfields that were planted here have attracted more deer to the area. I have even seen coyotes. New hunting laws help protect these animals."

Chet has always liked animals. He learned as much as he could about animals in high school and college. "I really enjoy this job because I help provide a home for animals. A few years ago we wanted to attract more Canada geese to this area. We built places for the geese to nest. We cleaned the lake and raised crops for the geese to eat. What was the result of our work? We now get 15,000 geese a year!"

Students often like to look at and read about animals—especially furry animals. When you think of a career with animals, you might think of a veterinarian—or animal doctor. But you can work with animals in other jobs too.

If a person is always being cruel to a pet dog, someone might call an **animal treatment investigator.** This person tries to make sure pets and other animals are not harmed by people. The investigator is like a police officer for animals. He or she also feeds starving animals and sets trapped animals free.

A **fish and game warden** also protects animals. Hunting and fishing is allowed in certain places and at certain times. The warden makes sure the fishers and hunters obey the laws.

A laboratory where scientists discover cures for diseases usually has some animals. The scientists test the drugs on animals before humans take them. An **animal technician** is in charge of caring for the animals in the laboratory. Technicians also assist veterinarians in an animal hospital.

To be an animal investigator, warden, or technician, you should like being around animals. But students who really want these jobs graduate from high school and study about animals in college.

Animal technician

Fish and game warden

On Your Own

Picture Clue

One of the science words on page 184 tells you about the picture on page 176.

Projects

1. Observe a bird gathering materials for making a nest. Make a list of the materials that blend with the bird's habitat and body covering. Draw a picture of the bird in its nest.

2. Write a report on how bees protect their hives. You can find this information in an encyclopedia.

3. Set up an aquarium. You can get directions and equipment at a pet store. Observe how the plants and animals live and grow in the aquarium.

Books About Science

Beware! These Animals Are Poison by Barbara Brenner. Coward, McCann & Geoghegan, 1979. Learn how animals use their poisons to protect themselves.

Find the Hidden Insect by Joanna Cole and Jerome Wexler. William Morrow and Company, 1979. Shows how insects hide themselves from their enemies.

Tooth and Claw; A Look at Animal Weapons by Russell Freedman. Holiday House, 1980. Find out how all kinds of animals protect themselves.

Unit Test

True or False

Number your paper from 1–5. Next to each number, write *true* if the sentence is correct and *false* if the sentence is incorrect. Make each false statement true by changing the underlined word and writing the correct word on your paper.

1. Predators cannot easily bite through a shrimp's <u>soft</u> outer covering.

2. A frog's color is its <u>camouflage</u>.

3. An eagle uses its <u>claws</u> to catch prey and to protect itself.

4. Some plants have parts covered with <u>poison</u>.

5. Bog plants get the nutrients they need from <u>soil</u>.

Matching

Number your paper from 6–10. Read the description in Column I. Next to each number, write the word from Column II that best matches the description in Column I.

Column I

6. the place where a plant or animal lives

7. hole dug in the ground by an animal

8. full of poison

9. an animal that hunts, kills, and eats other animals

10. an animal that is hunted for food

Column II

a. poisonous

b. habitat

c. predator

d. prey

e. burrow

f. camouflage

UNIT EIGHT
GREEN AND GROWING

Growing up,
   not down.
First green,
   then yellow.
Picked,
   then eaten.

Alice Antone *age 8*

Chapter 16
Food from Plants

People eat all these different parts of plants. Have you eaten some fruits, seeds, roots, stems, flowers, or leaves today?

The lessons in this chapter will show you some plants that you may not have seen growing. You may have seen parts of these plants in the grocery store.

1 Observing Foods from Plants

Do you know of a plant with a stem that grows underground? Have you ever seen grass as tall as you are? The picture shows foods from both types of plants. The white potato is an underground stem. The hamburger bun is made with flour from wheat—a tall grass.

Some of the other foods in the picture also come from plants. Find the foods from mustard seeds, cucumbers, cabbages, and orange trees. Think of ten other foods that you eat which come from plants. List the foods on paper. Next to each food, draw how you think the whole plant looks.

Think About It

1. What plant was named most often by students in your class?
2. **Challenge** From what plant does your favorite cereal come?

Foods made mainly from plants

2 What Fruits and Seeds Do People Eat?

fruit (früt), the part of a plant that holds the seeds.

Have You Heard?

Some seeds are used to make other foods taste better. Nutmeg and pepper are made from seeds that have been ground into a powder.

Most people think of apples, oranges, peaches, cherries, and strawberries as fruits. But tomatoes, cucumbers, string beans, and squash are also fruits. A **fruit** is the part of a flowering plant that has seeds. The picture shows some fruits that people eat. Find the seeds in the fruits.

Sometimes we eat only the seeds from a fruit. Sunflower seeds, peas, and lima beans are seeds that people eat.

Fruits have seeds

Not all parts of a plant are safe to eat—or **edible.** The fruit of the cherry tree in the picture is safe and good tasting. But the leaves and twigs could make you sick. It is important to know which parts of plants are edible.

Some plant parts are not safe to eat until they are cooked. Raw rhubarb leaves are poisonous, but cooked leaves are edible.

edible (ed′ə bəl), safe to eat.

Think About It

1. What is a fruit?
2. Name some seeds that people eat.
3. **Challenge** How would you find out if a plant part is a fruit?

Find Out

The tomato belongs to a family of plants called *Nightshade*. Use an encyclopedia to find out how all the plants in this family are alike.

Cherry tree

3 What Roots and Stems Do People Eat?

People eat other plant parts besides fruits. Look at the vegetable garden below. This drawing shows what some vegetables look like above ground and under the ground.

Eight different plants are growing in this garden. Notice the plants with thick roots. These plants store food in their roots. When you eat sweet potatoes, radishes, carrots, beets, and turnips, you are eating roots.

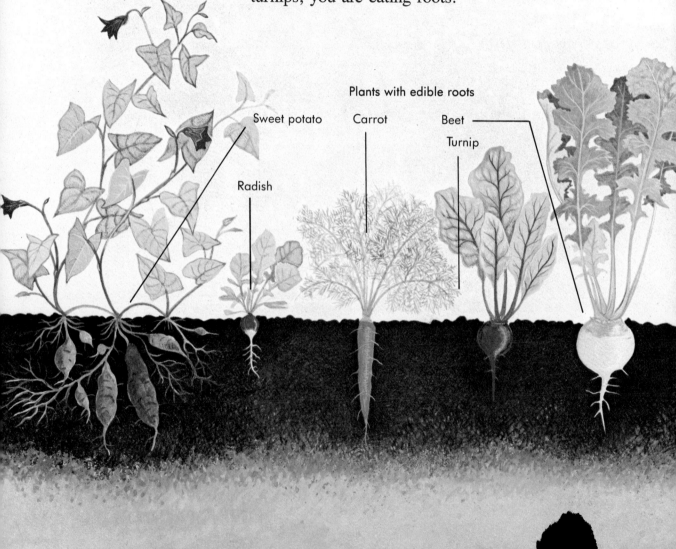

Plants with edible roots

Sweet potato

Carrot

Beet

Turnip

Radish

The plants shown below have edible stems. The stems of the asparagus (ə spar′ə gəs) and kohlrabi (kōl′rä′bē) plants grow above the ground. White potatoes are stems that grow underground. Potato plants store food in these stems.

Think About It

1. Name some plants with edible roots.
2. Name some plants with edible stems.
3. **Challenge** Name two root foods that also have edible leaves.

Plants with edible stems

Asparagus

Kohlrabi

White potato

4 What Leaves and Flowers Do People Eat?

People eat leaves and flowers of plants. Think about the last salad you ate. Did it have lettuce or cauliflower (kô′lə flou′ər) in it? The part of the lettuce plant we eat are its leaves. The part of the cauliflower plant we eat are its flower buds.

The garden in the picture is planted with leafy vegetables. See if you can find the lettuce, cabbage, spinach, and Brussels sprouts. Look for the vegetables that are flower buds—the cauliflower and broccoli (brok′ə lē).

Think About It

1. Name some plants with edible leaves.
2. Name some plants with edible flowers.
3. **Challenge** Explain how you might use flowers that are not edible.

Have You Heard?

People eat the flowers of zucchini squash. The flowers are usually deep fried.

Plants with edible leaves or flowers

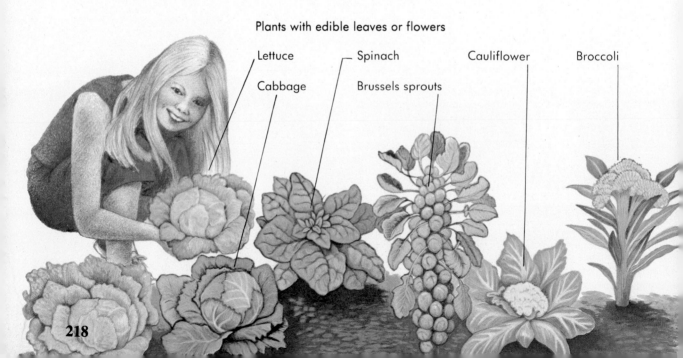

Lettuce

Cabbage

Spinach

Brussels sprouts

Cauliflower

Broccoli

Activity

Observing Edible Parts of Plants

Purpose
To observe which parts of plants are edible.

You Will Need
- samples of different parts of edible plants
- paper
- pencil
- crayons

Directions
1. Divide your paper into 6 parts as shown in the picture. Write *fruit, seed, root, stem, leaf,* or *flower* at the top of each part.
2. Look carefully at each sample of a plant part. Decide if it is a fruit, seed, root, stem, leaf, or flower.
3. Draw each plant part under the correct title as in the picture.

Think About It
1. Which part of your chart has the most samples?
2. Which part of your chart has the least samples?
3. **Challenge** Think of all the edible plants you can. Remember which part of each plant is edible. Now, invent a super plant with many edible parts. Draw a picture of your super plant.

Fruit	Seed	Root	Stem	Leaf	Flower

Do You Know?

Spices Are Made from Parts of Plants

Dill flowers

Nutmeg fruit and seed

Underground stem of ginger plant

How would you like to eat a flower for lunch? Maybe you never thought about eating flowers. But the flavor in your salad dressing or soup may come from flowers.

Many spices are made from flowers and other plant parts. Spices add flavor to foods. Some spices also make foods pleasant to smell. The pictures show some common spices.

The seeds of the dill plant are dried to make the spice called dill. You might have tasted dill in soups, salads, sauces, and pickles.

Two spices come from the nutmeg plant. The seed inside the fruit of this plant is used to make nutmeg. The red material covering the seed is made into a spice called mace. Nutmeg and mace add flavor to cakes, pies, meats, and vegetables.

Ginger is made from the underground stem of the ginger plant. The stem is dried and pounded into powder. Ginger is used to flavor desserts, pickles, and ginger ale.

Think of your favorite foods. Perhaps spices are added to these foods to make them tasty!

Tie It Together

Sum It Up

1. Look at the pictures of food. On a sheet of paper, write the numbers 1–5. Next to each number, tell what part of a plant each of the foods is from.

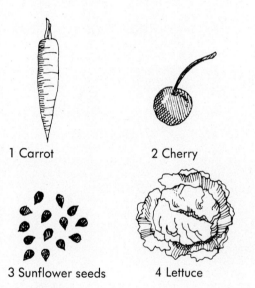

1 Carrot

2 Cherry

3 Sunflower seeds

4 Lettuce

5 Asparagus

Challenge

1. Make a list of your favorite fruits. Find out where in the United States they grow.

2. Name a drink made from a root.

3. How many different kinds of lettuce are sold at your grocery store?

4. Name the plant part that you eat most often.

Science Words

edible

fruit

Chapter 17
Uses of Plants

The tough, hard stem of a tree is used for food by termites. But people have other uses for trees. All of the objects in this picture came from the stems of trees.

The lessons in this chapter will show things you use which were once growing as plants.

1 Observing Different Uses of Paper

2 How Do People Use Trees?

3 How Do People Use Fibers?

1 Observing Different Uses of Paper

How much paper do you use in a day? You use a few pieces of paper to write on. You read words printed on paper. Maybe you brought your lunch to school in a paper bag.

Look around your classroom. See how many uses for paper you can find. List the uses on a sheet of paper. Then, think of the ways in which paper is used in your home. Add these uses to your list.

Think About It

1. What work do you do that uses the most paper?
2. **Challenge** Invent a new use for paper.

2 How Do People Use Trees?

Paper is made from trees. But paper is only one of the many useful things that people get from trees.

Wood is the hard, inner part of a tree's stem. The stem is covered by bark. Notice the trees in the pictures. The walnut has very hard, strong wood. Walnut wood is used to make furniture, paneling and pianos. The wood of the pine is strong but soft. Much of the paper and lumber that people use comes from pine trees. The soft, airy wood of the balsa is used to make model airplanes, boats, and cars.

Walnut tree

Pine tree

Balsa tree

You may have used maple syrup on pancakes. We make syrup from the liquid—or **sap**—of maple trees. Tiny tubes inside a tree carry sap from the roots to the leaves. Sap runs down from the bottom of a cut in the trunk into a pail, as shown in the picture. When the sap is boiled, it thickens into maple syrup.

Rubber also comes from the sap of a tree. **Latex** is the milky liquid of a rubber tree. It is collected in much the same way as maple sap. Then, it is made into rubber. Your bicycle tires and erasers might be made from rubber.

Chewing gum is made from the sap of a chicle (chik/əl) tree. The sap hardens into gum after it is taken from the tree. But the gum does not have much taste. Fruit or mint flavors are usually added to gum to give it a pleasing taste.

sap (sap), the water and minerals in a tree.

latex (lā/teks), a special substance found in the sap of many plants that is used to make rubber.

Find Out

Milkweed and dandelions have latex. Find out how people can change latex into rubber.

Sugar maple tree

Collecting maple syrup

225

How Do People Use the Bark of Trees?

Sometimes the bark on a tree is the useful part. Twice a year, growers carefully peel off and roll the bark of the cinnamon tree. Then, they cut it into cinnamon sticks. Some cinnamon bark is ground into powder. Many cooks use cinnamon powder to add flavor to foods, such as apple pie.

The bark of cork oak trees is used to make bottle stoppers, life preservers, flooring, and pin boards. Notice how the bark of the cork oak tree has been peeled and cut away. The tree will grow new layers of cork.

Think About It

1. Name three tree parts. Then, list some things made from each part.
2. **Challenge** Balsa wood is often used to make rafts that float on water. What property of balsa wood do you think makes it float?

Have You Heard?
The Chippewa Indians made canoes from the bark of birch trees.

Cork oak tree

Discover!

A Tree's Bark Can Be Useful

Bark-cloth tree

Imagine writing a letter on tree bark! American Indians wrote messages on birch tree bark. Baskets and cups were other objects they made from the bark of the birch tree. Birch bark was even stretched over wooden frames to make strong, light canoes.

While North American Indians rode in bark canoes, people in other parts of the world wore bark clothing. The picture shows one of the trees they used for cloth. People would soften and dye the bark. Then they made clothing, such as the skirt in the picture, from the bark cloth.

Another use of bark can be in making medicine. Bark from the

Bark-cloth skirt

cinchona tree is used in a medicine that has saved many lives. The medicine, quinine, is used to treat malaria.

Malaria is a disease carried by certain mosquitoes. Many people who are bitten by these mosquitoes become very sick and run a high fever.

Quinine helps bring down the fever and kill the organisms that cause the disease.

People have used bark to make quinine for hundreds of years. Today, doctors are studying tree bark to see if they can discover other useful medicines.

3 How Do People Use Fibers?

fiber (fī′bər), a stiff thread that holds up the parts of plants.

Have You Heard?

A cotton gin is a machine that separates the cotton fibers from the seeds. Oil from the cotton seeds is used for cooking and making soap.

Much of the cloth that people use for bedding, clothing, and towels comes from plants. The parts of plants are held up by stiff threads—or **fibers.** Some plant fibers can be used to make cloth. Notice the patterns of fibers in the cloth samples in the pictures.

People use strong fibers from the stems of flax plants to make thick cloth. The stems of these plants are dried, scraped, and combed into long, thin strips. The strips are spun into thread. Then, the thread is woven into linen cloth.

The fibers in cotton cloth come from inside the seed pod of the cotton plant. When the cotton is ripe, the pod pops open. The white, fuzzy fibers are then collected and made into cloth.

Flax plant

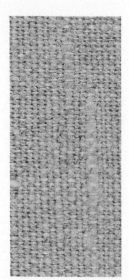

Linen cloth

Cotton plant

Cotton cloth

Rope can also be made from plant fibers. Notice the long leaves on the sisal (sis′əl) plant in the picture. These leaves are crushed and scraped with knives to remove their strong fibers. Then, the fibers are dried and twisted to make heavy string and rope.

Think About It

1. What part of a plant is usually made into cloth and rope?
2. **Challenge** What do you think would make a stronger rope, cotton or sisal? Why do you think so?

Sisal plant

Sisal rope

Activity

Looking at Fibers

Purpose
To compare the fibers in things made from parts of plants.

You Will Need
- hand lens
- papers of different weights
- cotton cloth
- cotton ball
- string
- rope
- flat wooden stick (broken into halves)
- paper plate
- pitcher of water colored with several drops of food coloring

Directions
1. Tear the papers and the cloth 2 ways—up and down and across. Look at the edges under the hand lens, as in the picture.
2. Look at each of the other samples under the hand lens.
3. Place an edge of each sample in a plate. Leave the other edge out of the plate, as in the picture.
4. Slowly pour some colored water into the plate until the water reaches the edges of the samples. Watch to see which sample soaks up the most water.

Think About It
1. What do the fibers look like?
2. Which fibers are the thickest?
3. Which samples soaked up water faster, the softer ones or the harder ones?
4. **Challenge** Nylon cloth is not made from plant fibers. Compare the fibers in nylon cloth with the fibers in the other samples.

Tie It Together

Sum It Up

Look at the room in the picture. Make a list of all the objects that come from plants.

Challenge!

1. Make a list of the different ways you can use newspaper.

2. What different kinds of wood were used to build the furniture in your home?

3. What objects in your home are made from plant fibers?

Science Words

fiber

latex

sap

Laboratory

Making New Paper from Used Paper

Purpose
To observe that used paper can be remade into fresh sheets.

You Will Need
- paper egg cartons
- large bowl
- liquid starch
- baking pan, about 23 cm × 31 cm
- 2 wire screens to fit in the pan
- masking tape
- eggbeater
- stacks of newspaper
- 2 cotton cloths
- piece of cardboard, about 25 cm × 35 cm
- books or heavy objects
- wooden board, about 25 cm × 35 cm

Stating the Problem
   All over the world, trees are cut down to make paper. Fibers from the tree's wood are soaked to make them soft. Then, the fibers are ground and pressed into sheets of paper. Think about all the ways you use paper. Some people worry that trees do not grow fast enough to keep up with all the paper people use. They would like people to use paper over again. How can this be done?

Investigating the Problem
1. Tear up the egg carton into small pieces. Make the pieces about the size of postage stamps. Put the pieces in a large bowl.
2. Pour liquid starch over the paper as in picture a. Pour in enough to cover the pieces. Allow the starch and paper to soak for 5 hours.
3. While you wait, cover the edges of your screens with masking tape to keep the edges from cutting you. Place one of the screens inside the pan. Fold the ends up as shown in picture b. You will hold onto the sides to lift the screening later.
4. After several hours have passed, use an eggbeater to beat up the paper-starch mixture. Beat until everything is completely mixed. See picture c. The mixture is now called pulp.

a

b

5. Pour the pulp into the pan. Swish the pulp back and forth across the screen. Do this until the pulp is evenly spread out in a thin layer.

6. Take 2 4-cm stacks of newspaper and cover each stack with a cotton cloth. You will use the newspaper and the cloth to blot the liquid from the newly made paper.

7. Slowly lift the screen out of the pan. Hold the screen over the pan for about 1 minute to let the liquid drain into the pan.

8. Put the screen on the newspaper and cloth blotter. Use the second piece of screen to press extra liquid from the pulp into the blotter. See picture *d.*

9. Carefully turn over the new sheet of paper and place it on the second newspaper and cloth blotter. Remove the screen. Place the unfolded screen on top of the newly made paper. Put a piece of cardboard on top of the screen. Cover the cardboard with a dry cotton cloth. Place some books or other heavy objects on top of the cloth. The weight of the books will press the extra liquid into the newspaper and cloth blotter. Let the paper sit for 15 minutes.

10. Remove the books, cloth, cardboard, and screen from the paper. The paper should be dry enough to peel off the blotter. Lay the new sheet of paper on a wooden board. Place the board in the sun. Let the paper dry in the sun for several hours.

11. Try writing on your paper. Use pencil, pen, crayon, and markers. Compare your writing on the paper to the way your writing looks on regular paper and on egg cartons.

Making Conclusions

1. How was the paper you made like the paper you started with?

2. How might paper made from old writing paper compare to the paper you made?

3. What material in the old paper gets reused when you make new paper?

4. List four kinds of paper that can be used and then made into new paper. List some kinds of paper that cannot be made into new paper.

c

d

Careers

Chef

"Without plants, I would be out of business," says Marcia. How does Marcia use plants in her work? She is a chef. "We use some plants in the cafeteria for decoration. But most of our customers prefer the kind of plants you eat, like fruits and vegetables."

Marcia started working in a restaurant with her father. "My father was a chef for thirty years. I started working with him when I was fourteen years old. My job was washing dishes. After high school, I went to college for two years. I learned how to cook and manage a restaurant. You do not have to go to college to become a chef, but it helps."

Now, Marcia is a chef and the manager of a cafeteria. "We feed about 2,000 people here a day. Of course, I do not cook for all of them. I have 25 people working for me in the kitchen. Some are cooks, some are bakers, and some are dishwashers. But they all work together to please our customers."

Besides helping to cook the food, Marcia also makes up the menu and orders the food. "At times, I talk with a dietician to make sure the meals we serve are nutritious.

"Cooking in a restaurant or cafeteria can be hard because you may have to work on holidays and at night. But I really enjoy it when I know that people liked something I made. They often compliment me on my work. That makes all my efforts worthwhile."

Every day, you probably use a plant or something that came from a plant. Wooden pencils and the paper in this book came from plants. Much of your food used to be growing plants.

Many people's jobs depend on plants. A **carpenter** could not work without using the largest plants in the world—trees. Carpenters use wood from trees to build houses and other things.

A carpenter knows a lot about different kinds of wood. He or she knows that certain kinds of wood are better for certain things. Carpenters have to know how and where to place wooden boards to construct a building properly. They do a lot of careful measuring.

Carpenters usually learn their skills in a special school after high school.

Another important use of plants is for medicines. Many **chemists** work in laboratories to make medicines from plants. Some chemists experiment with plants and other materials to find cures for diseases.

Students go to college to become chemists.

One of the most important uses of plants is for food. People all around the world depend on **farmers** to grow this food. Farmers know when to plant and harvest crops. They operate tractors and other large machines to help them in their work. Many farmers learn how to identify diseases that harm their crops.

Sometimes farmers take classes to learn more about soils, crops, and farming methods.

Carpenter

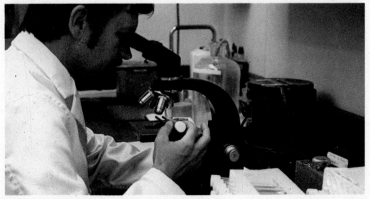

Chemist

On Your Own

Picture Clue

Look closely at the picture on page 210. Notice how the fruit is growing. This fruit is edible when the skin turns yellow. You might eat this fruit sliced on cereal.

Projects

1. Grow a sweet-potato plant from a root. Place the pointed end in a jar. Half fill the jar with water. New stems with leaves should grow in a few weeks. Add water when necessary.

2. Write a report on how Charles Goodyear discovered an improved way of making rubber. You can find the information in an encyclopedia.

3. Test the strength of the fibers in braided grass. First, try breaking a blade of grass. Then, braid several blades together, and try breaking the braid.

Books About Science

Eat the Fruit, Plant the Seed by Millicent E. Selsam and Jerome Wexler. William Morrow & Co., Inc., 1980. Learn what fruit seeds look like and how they look when they sprout. Also learn how you can care for young plants.

The Pumpkin People by David and Maggie Cavagnaro. Sierra, 1979. Find out how pumpkins are grown, and how they are used.

The Tremendous Tree Book by May Garelick and Barbara Brenner. Four Winds Press, 1979. Learn what makes a tree one of the most useful plants on earth.

Unit Test

True or False

Number your paper from 1–10. Next to each number, write *true* if the sentence is correct and *false* if the sentence is incorrect. Make each false statement true by changing the underlined word and writing the correct word on your paper.

1. A <u>stem</u> is the part of a flowering plant that has seeds.

2. <u>Some</u> plant parts are poisonous.

3. When you eat sweet potatoes, radishes, and carrots, you are eating <u>stems</u>.

4. People eat the <u>leaves</u> of a lettuce plant.

5. A white potato is a <u>leaf</u> that grows underground.

6. People eat the <u>flower</u> buds of a broccoli plant.

7. Maple syrup is made from the <u>sap</u> of a maple tree.

8. Pin boards are made from the <u>wood</u> of cork oak trees.

9. Cotton cloth is made from <u>fibers</u> inside the seed pod of a cotton plant.

10. <u>Latex</u> is a special substance that is found in the sap of many plants and is used to make rubber.

Glossary/Index

a hat	**i** it	**oi** oil	**ch** child	⎧ a in about
ā age	**ī** ice	**ou** out	**ng** long	⎪ e in taken
ä far	**o** hot	**u** cup	**sh** she	**ə** = ⎨ i in pencil
e let	**ō** open	**u̇** put	**th** thin	⎪ o in lemon
ē equal	**ô** order	**ü** rule	**ᴛʜ** then	⎩ u in circus
ėr term			**zh** measure	

air, in soil, 106, 110

animals
   and camouflage, 184–186
   defenses of, 189–194
   and fossils, 124–125
   and protective coverings, 179,
     180–183
   and soil, 108

attract (ə trakt′), 65, 74: pull to or
   toward

bar magnet, 64

bark, 226

blood, 6, 10, 16

body fat, 9, 17

bones, 7, 97, 124, 125

Brontosaurus (bron′tə sôr′əs), 135

burrow (bėr′ō), 191: hole dug in the
   ground by an animal

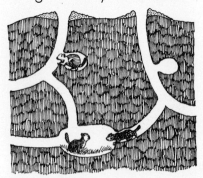
burrow

camouflage (kam′ə fläzh), 184–186: a
   color or pattern that keeps an
   animal from being easily seen

carbohydrate (kär′bō hī′drāt), 8–9: a
   sugar or starch that is used by
   the body for energy

cast (kast), 127: shape of an
   organism that is made by filling
   a hollow space

charge (chärj), 74–75, 76–77: a tiny
   bit of electricity

chicle (chik′əl), 225

circuit (sėr′kit), 77–78, 80, 81: the
   complete path that charges
   travel

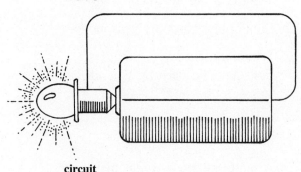
circuit

claws, 194

clay, 110–111

color
   and camouflage, 184–185
   of rainbow, 40–41
   of soil, 108, 110

compass (kum′pəs), 68–69, 70: an
   object that shows directions

condense (kən dens′), 152, 154–155:
   change from a gas into a liquid

coverings, of animals
   and camouflage, 184–185
   how they protect, 180–182
   observing, 179

coverings, of plants, 197–198

decay (di kā′), 108, 124: to slowly
   break down or rot

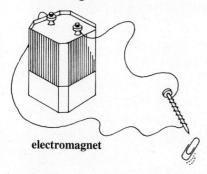

electromagnet

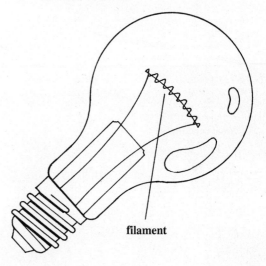

filament

a hat	i it	oi oil	ch child		a in about
ā age	ī ice	ou out	ng long		e in taken
ä far	o hot	u cup	sh she	ə =	i in pencil
e let	ō open	ù put	th thin		o in lemon
ē equal	ô order	ü rule	ᴛʜ then		u in circus
ėr term			zh measure		

fossil (fos′əl), 124: sign or evidence
of past life
and dinosaurs, 134–138
finding, 129–130
forming, 125–127
skeletons, 140

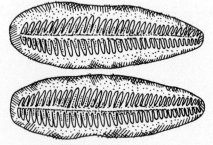

fossil fern leaves

fresh water, 162–163, 164: water
that contains very little salt
hard, soft, 168
fruit (früt), 214–215: the part of a
plant that holds the seeds

fruit (pear)

granite (gran′it), 95, 96
graphite (graf′īt), 94
groundwater, 163: water that fills the
spaces between and within
pieces of rock underground

habitat (hab′ə tat), 181, 197, 200: the
place where a plant or animal
lives
hard water, 168: water that contains
a lot of minerals
heart
and exercise, 16, 19
and sleep, 18
human body
and exercise, 16–17, 19
need for sleep, 18
nutrients needed in, 6–12
protecting skin, 20–21
humus (hyü′məs), 108, 110: decayed
matter that gives soil nutrients
and a dark color
igneous (ig′nē əs) **rock,** 96: rock that
forms from melted minerals
image (im′ij), 35: likeness or copy
infer (in fėr′), 134, 139: to use what
you already know to make a
careful guess
lakes, 97, 159, 162
latex (lā′teks), 225: a special
substance found in the sap of
many plants that is used to
make rubber
light
brightness of, 38–39
changing directions, 34–35
and fireflies, 42
how it travels, 33
and plant growth, 200
and shadows, 36–37
and spectrum, 40–41
light bulb, 76–77
like poles, 66: poles that are the
same
lodestone, 62

magnetic (mag net′ik), 68: having the properties of a magnet

magnetic poles, 64–66, 68, 82

magnetism (mag′nə tiz′əm), 64: the push or pull of a magnet
and compasses, 68–69, 70
and electricity, 74, 80–82

magnets, 63, 64–66, 81
and poles, 64–66, 68, 82

maple syrup, 225

matter (mat′ər), 47: anything that takes up space and has weight
in soil, 106

metamorphic (met′ə môr′fik) **rock,** 98: igneous or sedimentary rock whose minerals have been changed by heat and pressure

mica (mī′kə), 95

mineral (min′ər əl), 8, 10: a nutrient that helps the body work at its best

mineral (min′ər əl), 94–95, 126: a material that forms from matter that was never alive
mining, 100–101
naming properties of, 93
and plant growth, 200
and water, 160–161, 168

mineral (diamond)

mines, 100–101

mold (mold), 127: a print left in a rock by a decayed organism

muscles, 7, 18
exercising, 16–17, 19
testing power of, 15

north pole, 65–66, 68–69

northern lights, 79

nutrient (nü′trē ənt), 6–7: a substance that is needed for health and growth
six kinds of, 8–10
in soil, 108, 111
needed by plants, 108

oceans, 97, 159, 161

ocean floor, 97, 127

opaque (ō pāk′), 37: not letting light through

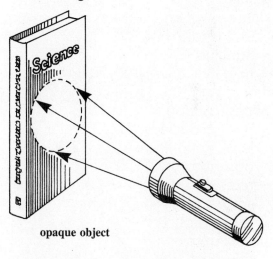

opaque object

ore (ôr), 100–101: rock that contains enough of a useful mineral to make it worth mining
in bicycles, 102

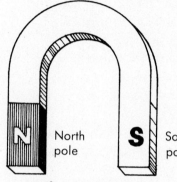

river, 97, 159, 162–163
rocks
    identifying, 99
    and minerals, 94–95
    and mining, 100–101
    and salt water, 161
    and soil, 106–108
    three kinds of, 96–98
roots, 216–217, 225
salt, 160–161
salt water, 160–161, 164: water that
    contains a lot of salt
sand, 106, 110–111
sap (sap), 225: the water and
    minerals in a tree
scales, 181
sea organisms, and fossils, 127, 128
sediment (sed′ə mənt), 97, 127: bits of
    rock and other material that sink
    to the bottom of a river, lake, or
    ocean
sedimentary (sed′ə men′tər ē) **rock,**
    97, 130: rock that forms from
    sediment being pressed together

sedimentary rock

seeds, 214
shadows, 36–37
shell, of animal, 180
shellfish, 127, 180
sisal (sis′əl) , 229

skin, 7
    artificial, 22
    protecting, 20–21
    as a protection, 179–181
sleep, need for, 18
snacks, 5, 7
soft water, 168: water that contains
    few or no minerals
soil
    different kinds of, 110–111
    examining, 105
    forming, 106–108
    and plant growth, 201
    and police work, 109
    and water, 106–108, 111, 112
sound
    and bats, 49
    different levels of, 50–51
    and echo, 48
    making, 45
    predicting, 47, 52
sound waves, 46–47
source (sôrs), 34, 46: thing from
    which anything comes
south pole, 65–66, 68–69
spectrum (spek′trəm), 40–41: the
    band of colors formed when a
    beam of white light is broken up

Red
Orange
Yellow
Green
Blue
Indigo
Violet

spectrum

a hat	i it	oi oil	ch child		a in about
ā age	ī ice	ou out	ng long		e in taken
ä far	o hot	u cup	sh she	ə =	i in pencil
e let	ō open	ù put	th thin		o in lemon
ē equal	ô order	ü rule	ᴛʜ then		u in circus
ėr term			zh measure		

stems, 200, 202, 213, 216–217, 224, 228

stomach, 6

sunburn, 21

surface (sėr′fis), 35, 96, 163: the outside of anything

teeth, 6, 124, 125, 194

translucent (tran slü′snt), 36: stops some light, but not enough for shadows to be seen

transparent (tran sper′ənt), 36: lets light through

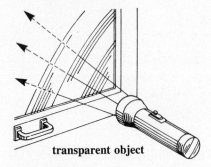

transparent object

trees, 200, 224–226

Tyrannosaurus (ti ran′ə sôr′əs), 137

unlike poles, 65, 82: poles that are opposites

vibrate (vī′brāt), 46, 50–51: move rapidly back and forth

vitamin (vī′tə mən), 8, 10: a nutrient that is needed in small amounts for normal growth and health of the body

volcano, 96

water
  fresh, 162–163, 168
  groundwater, 163
  hard, soft, 168
  as a nutrient, 8, 10
  observing, 151
  pathways of, 159
  and plant growth, 200
  protecting our supply, 166–167
  salt, 160–161, 164
  and soil, 106–108, 111, 112
  stored in plants, 197
  traveling to your home, 165

water cycle (sī′kəl), 155, 156: path that water takes as it moves from one place to another

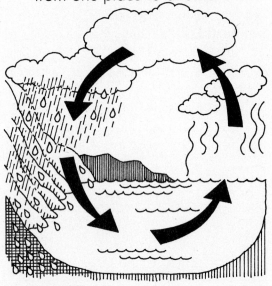

water cycle

water vapor (vā′pər), 152, 154–155: water in the air that is in the form of a gas

wood, 126, 224

woolly mammoth, 124

Acknowledgments

Positions of photographs are shown in abbreviated form as follows: top (t), bottom (b), center (c), left (l), right (r). All photographs not credited are the property of Scott, Foresman and Company. Cover, illustration by William Peterson, photograph by David Muench; **2,** Robert McKendrick; **4, (all)** NASA; **16, (l)** Larry West, **(r)** Marion Bernstein; **21,** Richard Hutchings/Photo Researchers; **22,** Dan McCoy/Rainbow; **26,** Melanie Shafer/Globe Photos; **27,** USDA; **30,** Everett C. Johnson; **40,** Grant Heilman; **42, (t)** E. R. Degginger, **(b)** Ivan Polunin/Bruce Coleman Inc.; **46, (t)** David G. Fitzgerald/After Image; **49,** S. C. Bisserôt/Bruce Coleman Inc.; **56,** Cameramann Internat'l.; **57, (l)** E. R. Degginger; **60,** Michael Philip Manheim/Photo Researchers; **67,** John Gerard; **75, (inset)** Thomas Ives; **79, 81, (inset)** E. R. Degginger; **87, (r)** Chris Reeberg/DPI; **90,** Matt Brown/West Stock; **92,** Pierre Boulat/Cosmos, Paris; **94, (lc, r)** E. R. Degginger, **(rc)** Jerome Wyckoff; **96,** Gianni Tortoli/Photo Researchers, **(inset)** John Running; **97,** Phil Degginger; **98, (l)** E. R. Degginger, **(r)** Peyton Hoge/Corn's Photo; **100–101,** Alan Pitcairn/Grant Heilman; **102,** Cameramann Internat'l.; **104,** USDA; **105, (both)** John Messineo; **106, (l)** Edward S. Ross; **108,** Grant Heilman; **109,** François Duhamel/Mega; **111, (inset)** Grant Heilman; **116,** Cameramann Internat'l.; **117, (l)** Al Stephens/Corn's Photo, **(r)** Cameramann Internat'l.; **120,** E. R. Degginger; **124,** Wide World; **125,** Manfred Kage/Peter Arnold, Inc; **126,** Lois and George Cox/Bruce Coleman Inc.; **127, (l)** Louise K. Broman/Root Resources; **129, (l)** Stewart M. Green/Tom Stack & Assoc., **(r)** Allan Roberts; **130, (b)** Michael Collier; **132,** Courtesy Museum of Science, Boston; **134, (l)** Paläotologisches Museum, Museum für Naturkunde der Humboldt-Universität, Berlin, DDR; **136,** By courtesy of the Trustees, British Museum (Natural History); **138, (t)** Dinosaur State Park, Conn.; **(b)** Field Museum of Natural History, Chicago; **140,** Vince Abromitis, photographer, courtesy of Carnegie Museum of Natural History; **143, (r)** Adam Woolfitt/Woodfin Camp & Assoc.; **144,** Michael Collier; **145, (l)** Georg Gerster/Photo Researchers; **148,** Gene Ahrens; **150,** Jerome Wyckoff; **153,** Ardea London; **154,** Frank J. Miller/Photo Researchers; **158, (l)** H. Hasen-Harza/Root Resources; **158–159,** David Muench; **159, (inset)** J. D. Taylor/Valan Photos; **160–161,** Fritz Henle/Photo Researchers; **161, (inset)** Tom Stack & Assoc.; **162, (l)** Stephen J. Krasemann/DRK Photo, **(r)** Michael Collier; **166, (l)** Phil Degginger, **(tc, tr)** Tom Myers, **(b)** Douglas Faulkner/Photo Researchers; **168,** Sally Myers; **173, (b)** Carl Roessler/Alpha-FPG; **176,** E. R. Degginger; **178,** Norman Lightfoot/Photo Researchers;

179, (l) E. R. Degginger, **(r)** Margot Conte/Animals Animals; **181, (t)** R. Andrew Odum/Peter Arnold, Inc., **(bl)** R. S. Virdee/Grant Heilman, **(br)** E. R. Degginger; **182, (l)** Stephen J. Krasemann/DRK Photo, **(r)** E. R. Degginger; **183,** Wayne Lankinen/Valan Photos; **184, (l)** Perry D. Slocum/Animals Animals, **(r)** Stan Wayman/Photo Researchers; **185, (l)** Leonard Lee Rue III/Photo Researchers, **(r)** Edward S. Ross; **188,** Jane Burton/Bruce Coleman Inc.; **189, (t)** Anthony Mercieca/Root Resources, **(bl)** Jim Brandenburg, **(br)** Sven-Olaf Lindblad/Photo Researchers; **190, (l)** Charles Palek/Animals Animals, **(r)** Robert L. Dunne/Bruce Coleman Inc.; **191,** Tom McHugh/Photo Researchers; **193,** Tom Brakefield; **194,** James Hancock/Photo Researchers; **196,** Wardene Weisser/Ardea London; **197, (l)** David Muench, **(r)** Ronald F. Thomas/Bruce Coleman Inc.; **198, (t)** P. Morris/Ardea London, **(c)** John Gerard, **(br)** Bruce Coleman/Bruce Coleman Inc.; **199, (l)** Shirley Hawn/Taurus Photos; **200, (l)** Tom McHugh/Photo Researchers, **(r)** Charles R. Belinky/Photo Researchers; **201, (both)** Hans Pfletschinger/Peter Arnold, Inc.; **205, (l)** E. R. Degginger, **(r)** Wayne Lankinen/DRK Photo; **206,** Tim Irwin/Uniphoto; **207, (r)** U.S. Fish & Wildlife Service, photo by Steve Van Riper; **210,** Edward S. Ross; **215, (t inset)** Yvonne Freund/Photo Researchers; **220, (t,c)** W. H. Hodge, **(b)** W. H. Hodge/Peter Arnold, Inc.; **222, (t)** Debbie Dean, **(c)** Harry Hartman/Bruce Coleman Inc., **(bl)** Timothy H. Sharp/Earth Images; **224–225** Grant Heilman; **224, (l inset)** Tom McHugh/Photo Researchers, **(c inset)** George Kleiman/Photo Researchers, **(r inset)** W. H. Hodge/Peter Arnold, Inc.; **225, (l)** Clyde H. Smith/Peter Arnold, Inc., **(r)** J. D. Markou/Valan Photos; **226,** Virginia Carleton/Photo Researchers; **227, (t)** Harper Horticultural Slide Library, **(b)** Field Museum of Natural History, Chicago; **228, (l)** Grant Heilman, **(rc)** Alan Pitcairn/Grant Heilman; **229, (l)** Robert Mitchell/Earth Scenes.

We wish to express our appreciation to the following schools for their contributions:

Poems for the series were written by children at Fairfield Public Schools, Fairfield, Connecticut; Greeley School, Winnetka, Illinois; Howland School, Chicago, Illinois; Indian Oasis Elementary District, Sells, Arizona; and Model Laboratory School, Eastern Kentucky University, Richmond, Kentucky.

Cloze reading tests for the series were administered at Banting Elementary School, Waukesha, Wisconsin; and Gospel Lutheran Grade School, Milwaukee, Wisconsin.

Photographs for Book 3 were taken at Orrington School, Evanston, Illinois; and Martin Luther King Lab School, Evanston, Illinois.

Using Metric

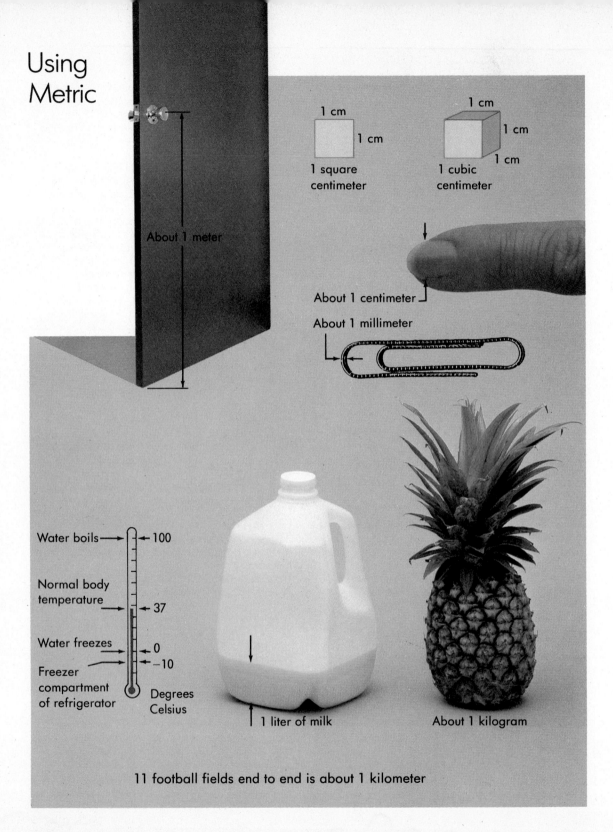

About 1 meter

1 cm 1 cm
1 square centimeter

1 cm 1 cm 1 cm
1 cubic centimeter

About 1 centimeter

About 1 millimeter

Water boils → ← 100

Normal body temperature → ← 37

Water freezes → ← 0

Freezer compartment of refrigerator → ← −10

Degrees Celsius

1 liter of milk

About 1 kilogram

11 football fields end to end is about 1 kilometer